ILLUSTRATORS
ANNUAL **2020**

BOLOGNA CHILDREN'S BOOK FAIR
ILLUSTRATORS EXHIBITION

Illustrators selected by

VALÉRIE CUSSAGUET
ENRICO FORNAROLI
LORENZO MATTOTTI
CATHY OLMEDILLAS
MACHIKO WAKATSUKI

CHRONICLE BOOKS
SAN FRANCISCO

An event by:

President
GIANPIERO CALZOLARI

General Manager
ANTONIO BRUZZONE

Culture Business Unit Director
MARCO MOMOLI

Exhibition Manager
ELENA PASOLI

Bologna Children's Book Fair
Show Office
MARZIA SAMPAOLI
CRISTINA PANCALDI
PAOLA LACCHINI
ISABELLA DEL MONTE
ALICE NATALI

Illustrators Exhibition
DEANNA BELLUTI
SERENA PRATI

Bologna Children's Book Fair
Viale della Fiera, 20
40127 Bologna, Italy
www.bolognachildrensbookfair.com
bookfair@bolognafiere.it
illustratori@bolognafiere.it

BolognaFiere s.p.a. and Maurizio Corraini s.r.l.
do not assume responsibility for omissions,
incorrect information or descriptions,
oversights or errors in respect
to the information contained herein.

ILLUSTRATORS
ANNUAL 2020

CONTENTS

HASSAN MOUSAVI

**COVER ARTIST
OF THE ILLUSTRATORS
ANNUAL 2020**

The Bratislava Illustration Biennial that awarded your book *The Boxer* highlighted your way of using "words and pictures to familiarize children with a culture of peace while creating dynamic images that carry a deep moral message." Do you agree with that? How important is it for you to make a moral point through your work?

In my opinion, despite what we expected, we live in a world full of rage, war and inhumane relationships. Unfortunately technology and human development haven't led to peace. This book has a message for children, to avoid what we have done to our planet. Life teaches us many important, effective and practical lessons. I have attempted to relate what I have learned in my life in the form of a children's story. *The Boxer*, published by TUTI in 2017, revolves around concepts of peace and unity: how to avoid destruction and desolation, and to try not to slavishly pursue the success of others. The boxer is an ordinary person who becomes famous, wealthy and successful. He gradually forgets human values. In his fast-forward movement toward prosperity, he pauses and thinks about his goal. Then he learns a lesson that he tries to teach to his students as well: "When you raise your fist, it is important to know where to punch."

Can you name three influences, inside or outside the illustration world, that have shaped your work as an artist and illustrator?

In 2005, one of the golden eras of Iranian illustration, when I had started my career in that field, there were several outstanding talents, such as Farshid Shafiee, Morteza Zahedi, Ali Boozari, Rashin Kheyrieh, Amir Shabanipour . . . They played a vital role in forming Iranian illustration as we now know it. Their works had an impact on novice illustrators, especially those like me who learned the art of illustration by observing their works, without any masters.

However, when I first made the acquaintance of Květa Pacovská, I was deeply engrossed by her personality and the charisma of her works, which always convey the powerful beauty of colors.

Other illustrators, such as Saul Steinberg, Brad Holland and Ralph Steadman, have also stunned me. But if you ask me to name the most effective one, I would still say it is Květa Pacovská.

BOXER. FROM "THE BOXER." TUTI BOOKS. TEHRAN. 2017

6

Hassan Mousavi (Iran, 1983), Iranian painter and illustrator, was born in a middle class family in Qom. During his childhood he began making things in his father's metal workshop. Small pieces of iron with different shapes were the first subjects of his illustrations. Drawing and creating super-humans who would save the world was his childhood pastime. Instead of becoming a blacksmith as planned, he became familiar with graphic design, which opened up new perspectives in his life, of which illustration became the central focus. He continued his education in graphic design at Shahid Beheshti University in Karaj. Artists such as Farshid Mesqali, Květa Pacovská and Štěpán Zavřel inspired his work. He has illustrated over 40 children's books for various publishers around the world, and his artworks have been shown in Iran, Germany, Denmark, Japan, Czech Republic, Slovakia, Italy and UAE. His illustrations were selected for the Illustrators Exhibition 2013 of the Bologna Children's Book Fair. In 2018, he received the honor diploma from the Children's Book Council of Iran (IBBY-Iran). *The Boxer*, which he wrote and illustrated, was included in the White Ravens list in 2018, and he received the Grand Prix BIB (Biennial of Illustration Bratislava) for this book in 2019. He uses words and pictures to familiarize children with the culture of peace, and creates dynamic images that carry a profound moral message.

Since childhood, you have worked in your father's metalworking shop. Did this influence your work as an illustrator in any way?

Definitely. The characters of my first stories were screwdriver sets, the monster chainsaw, a milling machine, a bolt cutter with its mysterious form, and those tiny or big metal pieces that had their own personalities and features. So my first stories were mostly inspired by my father's workshop.

In recent years, it has become quite usual to find amazing Iranian illustrators among the selected artists in the BCBF Illustrators Exhibition. Is there any explanation for this fertility of the Iranian illustration tradition?

The art of illustration in Iran has its roots in our culture. In fact, Iranian painting developed through illustration of Persian classic texts, such as the *Shahnameh* and the *Khamseh* in manuscript form, in the Persian courts. Later came the establishment of organizations like the Institute for the Intellectual Development of Children and Young Adults (founded in 1961), leading to a contemporary approach

to children's books. This attitude existed until 1979, i.e. the Islamic Revolution, and it introduced prominent illustrators to the world and attracted the global attention. Then the Iran-Iraq war and its consequences slowed down this progress. The Tehran International Biennial of Illustration (TIBI, founded in 1990) brought about a specific change in Iranian illustration. It resulted in the founding of publishing houses with an approach of producing fine picture books, the formation of the Cultural/Artistic Society of Iranian Illustrators, followed by a notable presence of Iranian illustrators in the 2000s.

This history proves that Iranian illustrators are creative, active, diligent and gifted. So their books are translated into many languages and their remarkable works always stand out in international fairs.

Is there any Iranian artist who has been important for you and who, in your opinion, has gotten too little international attention outside your country?
Yes. Apart from those mentioned above, I know artists making work of high quality that are to some extent not visible, such as Mahdi Karimzadeh and Mahmud Khan (self-taught).

Would you explain something more about the creative process of the cover illustration of the 2020 Illustrators Annual? Please tell us about your initial idea and how it changed (if it changed) while you were working on it, the technique you have chosen, the problems you encountered . . .

The first sketch I did for the cover of the catalogue looked pretty similar to the final one! Of course I made other sketches as well, but I was sure that the right idea had occurred to me in the very first one. I chose to work on canvas, though most of my works are drawn on wood, for two reasons: First, if I drew a picture of that size on wood, it would be fragile; second, considering my idea, the canvas offers some essential facilitations. Fortunately everything went smoothly through the whole process.

The story of the cover begins with a sunrise and the appearance of a town that bears signs of the classical architecture of Italy. A town that hosts fictional characters from east and west, from various cultures in different parts of the world. They are either fictional characters in their own right, or they are reading books amidst the illustrated yet inseparable buildings. These characters invite the audience to delve into colors and textures, to seek and find images.

This magnificent day ends with a sunset and the return of the travelers. Then with the next day's sunrise a new story will take form, and another journey begins.

MR. GUARDIAN. FROM "MR. GUARDIAN." SORE-YE MEHR. TEHRAN. 2014
PREVIOUS PAGE: THE GOLDEN FISH. FROM "THE GOLDEN FISH."
INSTITUTE FOR THE INTELLECTUAL DEVELOPMENT OF CHILDREN AND YOUNG ADULTS. KANOON. 2017

A GRAND FRESCO
BOLOGNA ILLUSTRATORS EXHIBITION

For the 2020 edition of the Illustrators Exhibition, works arrived in Bologna by 2,574 artists from 66 countries, for a total of 12,870 panels. These were examined by a jury composed of five authoritative representatives of the various facets of the world of illustration and picture books: two publishers of reference in their countries—Valérie Cussaguet (France) and Machiko Wakatsuki (Japan)—an internationally renowned illustrator—Lorenzo Mattotti (Italy)—a founder and art director of magazines for young readers—Cathy Olmedillas (United Kingdom)—and a scholar in this field—Enrico Fornaroli (Italy).

The implications of coming to terms with such a mountain of materials are splendidly narrated in the jury's report, which traces back through the initial doubts, the criteria that gradually emerged for the selection, the phases of deliberation and, above all, the intentions that guided the choice: to make the catalogue "represent a wide variety of styles, different cultural and geographic expressions, not moving in a single direction but managing to convey the variety and trends of contemporary illustration." Because this was the task at hand: to create a fresco that would be as varied and representative as possible of what the world of illustration for children offers today.

The selection certainly lives up to the promise of geographical and cultural variety: Just consider the fact that the 76 artists chosen for the exhibition come from 23 different countries and regions: Italy, France, Korea, Japan, Argentina, China, Poland, Spain, Lithuania, Hong Kong, Germany, Finland, Taiwan, Chile, Russia, Netherlands, Uruguay, Iran, USA, Czech Republic, Switzerland, the United Kingdom and Peru.

To grasp the stylistic and technical variety of the selected works, you need only peruse the pages of this catalogue for a firsthand impression of the wealth of techniques, perspectives, sensibilities and approaches that coexist inside it. Among the chosen artists, you will find already successful exponents with a solid professional background, but also very young artists making their first appearance on the international stage. The task of the jury is to put the spotlight on the best artists, and above all "to discover the potential of young artists, fresh out of school, perhaps, and still needing time to mature," while the job of the exhibition as an institution is to bring out the value of these talents, offering them international visibility. This happens first in the exhibition, which is a central feature of the Bologna Children's Book Fair—a reference point for the entire children's book industry—then in the various stages of the long tour that takes the show around the world, and finally in this catalogue with international distribution.

MONTEVIDEO. 2020

SEOUL. 2020

The Illustrators Exhibition is fertile ground, which in its continuous evolution gives rise to a range of different initiatives. Here, we would like to mention two of them: first, the International Award for Illustration of BCBF and Fundación SM, now at its tenth iteration. Aimed at artists under 35 who have already been selected for the Illustrators Exhibition, the award offers the winner—selected by a jury of outstanding personalities in the world of illustration—a check for $15,000, with the aim of providing resources for one year of work on an illustrated album that will be published and launched on the worldwide market by the Spanish publishing house SM. The next album that will be presented at the BCBF is *Lucilla*, created by Sarah Mazzetti, winner of the award in 2019.

The second initiative we would like to mention is the project "BCBF Visual Identity Workshop." Since 2017, BCBF has chosen a young artist from the many talents of the Illustrators Exhibition to construct the visual universe of the next edition, under the creative direction of the design studio, Chialab. This year, the team of the Fair, together with Chialab, which has created the visual identity of BCBF practically every year since 2009, selected the Lithuanian illustrator Rasa Jančiauskaitė from the ranks of the artists included in the Illustrators Exhibition 2019.

Both in the case of the International Award for Illustration of BCBF-Fundación SM and in that of the project "BCBF Visual Identity Workshop," the originals of the illustrations produced will then be shown in two solo shows, first at the Fair and then in the various travels of the Exhibition throughout the world.

MONTEVIDEO. 2020

SEOUL. 2020

BUONOS AIRES. 2019

**ILLUSTRATORS EXHIBITION
INTERNATIONAL TOUR**

The Illustrators Exhibition of the Bologna Children's Book Fair is the highlight of an event that is unique in the world, not just as a very lively market for usage rights, but also as an effervescent creative workshop and international showcase for the latest trends in the field of children's illustration.

After Bologna, the Illustrators Exhibition travels on a two-year tour offering the selected illustrators truly worldwide visibility.

The stops include Japan, Korea and China, with the regular addition of other destinations, such as Argentina and Uruguay for the Illustrators Exhibition 2019, for example.

Thanks to over thirty years of friendship with JBBY—the Japanese Board on Books for Young People—the Illustrators Exhibition has become a traditional appointment in Japan, eagerly awaited by sector professionals as well as children who visit the show by the thousands, with their families or in school groups.

Here are the Japanese stops of the Illustrators Exhibition 2020:

HYOGO
NISHINOMIYA CITY OTANI MEMORIAL ART MUSEUM
4 JULY – 16 AUGUST 2020

TOKYO
ITABASHI ART MUSEUM
22 AUGUST – 27 SEPTEMBER 2020

MIE
YOKKAICHI MUNICIPAL MUSEUM
3 OCTOBER – 1 NOVEMBER 2020

ISHIKAWA
ISHIKAWA NANAO ART MUSEUM
6 NOVEMBER – 13 DECEMBER 2020

GUNMA
ART MUSEUM AND LIBRARY. OTA
19 DECEMBER – 24 JANUARY 2021

After Japan, the exhibition heads for Seoul, Korea, and then moves on to China, where it will be seen in three cities.

"GIVING LIFE TO CHILDREN'S CONTENT": THE VISUAL IDENTITY OF THE BOLOGNA CHILDREN'S BOOK FAIR 2020

Since 2017, the Bologna Children's Book Fair has entrusted a young artist selected from the many talents in the Illustrators Exhibition with the task of constructing the visual universe of the upcoming edition of the Fair, under the creative direction of the design studio, Chialab. This happens each year in the context of the project "BCBF Visual Identity Workshop," an intense laboratory of co-design that begins in the spring and makes its first public appearance in the fall.

After Daniele Castellano (Italy), Chloé Alméras (France) and Masha Titova (Russia), the protagonist of this fourth edition of the "Visual Identity Workshop" is the Lithuanian illustrator Rasa Jančiauskaitė, selected from the artists included in the Illustrators Exhibition 2019.

"Icastic, primordial, monochromatic, symbolic" are the four words that sum up the visual identity for 2020 of a fair that is a gathering place and an incubator of ideas that fosters sharing and borrowing, stimulating reproduction. Rasa Jančiauskaitė interprets these words through the egg-idea: to grant life, to shed light, to bring to birth, to nurse, to incubate and to return to the origin of representation, to the primordial, without anything more, without colors. Drawing as the primal moment whose sharing can give rise to new worlds, with the plus of a subtle touch of irony: "Giving Life to Children's Content."

CHIALAB is a design studio that works on visualization of information on paper, in spaces and on screens. It creates visual identities, tools and processes for their management. It designs and develops systems of publication and reading for digital publishing. The studio willingly shares its experience through teaching. (chialab.it)

RASA JANČIAUSKAITĖ, Lithuanian, born in 1991, earned a degree at the Vilnius Academy of Arts in Graphic Design and Visual Communication Design. She also took part in the Erasmus program at ISIA in Urbino and École Estienne in Paris. She presently works as a graphic designer, freelance illustrator and teacher of graphic design, while focusing on illustration projects for personal research or projects connected with picture books for children and young people. Rasa's published titles are: *Signs of Silence Book*, Dwie Siostry, Warsaw, 2016; *Small Poems for Little Ones*, Tikra knyga, Vilnius, 2018; *Say It in Sign Language*, Dwie Siostry, Warsaw, 2019.

19

ILLUSTRATORS
EXHIBITION
JURY REPORT

Taking part in the jury of the Illustrators Exhibition is like being thrust into a science fiction film in which a group of scientists, with different types of expertise and backgrounds, is closed inside a secret, isolated laboratory with just three days to find the antidote to a lethal extraterrestrial micro-organism, thus averting planetary catastrophe.

Precisely along these lines, *The Andromeda Strain* effect grips each juror upon entering the enormous pavilion/hangar containing the array of 2,574 dossiers of the candidates of the 2020 edition, carefully subdivided by type, nationality and category for a total of over 12,870 illustrations. An overwhelming sight at first, which conveys the enormity of the titanic task that lies ahead.

Nevertheless, from the first day onward, the jury proceeded with apparent calm, in a mixture of rash temerity and strong determination to meet and conquer the challenge presented by the Bologna Children's Book Fair to a quintet of "sector professionals:" two publishers operating on the front lines in their countries, one world-famous illustrator, one editor of children's magazines and one director of an academy with a focus on this discipline. An assorted team, hailing from France, Japan, Great Britain and Italy.

On the first day, after the ritual of introductions and operative recommendations, the group began to indicate its first choices, using colored stickers, as the result of relaxed, solitary browsing through the thousands of works, from which

75–80 selected candidates had to emerge. Silent glances between jurors, fleeting glimpses of the choices of their neighbors, a slow definition of personal criteria of evaluation, all gradually led to the first inevitable process of exclusion.

On the second day, the sea of images was still boundless, the colored flags had multiplied, but each juror still had plenty of sticky notes with which to express interest. The phase of discussion began, a dialogue addressing the merits of the first individual choices. In a slow procession along the tables covered with images, the team lingered over those that had received at least one colored sticker. The five jurors began to compare their impressions, explaining their assessment criteria, the principles through which progressive choices would determine which artists to insert in the exhibition and the catalogue.

Some criteria of selection were unanimous: The jurors were not simply looking for beautiful images, though the aesthetic aspect is fundamental, but rather for images that sum up the universe of their maker, defining a style, transmitting a vital energy while revealing a deeper, almost explosive narrative balance. Works that did not seem to be limited to the five submitted illustrations, but pointed to the possibility of further development. Other shared principles, which were formulated along the way, had to do with the need for the catalogue to represent a wide variety of styles, different cultural and geographic expressions, not moving in a single

21

direction but managing to convey the variety and trends of contemporary illustration. The selection had to discover the potential of young artists, fresh out of school, perhaps, and still needing time to mature.

It was in this phase that, from a serious indication to an amusing quip, a passionate debate to liberating laughter, the five jurors were transformed into a close-knit panel.

The third day was that of the final selection, in which the circle had to be closed, sharing in the choices of the others or fiercely insisting that a particular work "absolutely must remain" while another "necessarily must be excluded" from the ranks of the chosen group. This was a day of fine-tuning, emphasizing the focus on illustration and children's liter-

ature, the need for the images to have an effective narrative rhythm, an ironclad composition, while containing the concept for an illustrated book.

This was the day, finally, in which the jury managed to give concrete form, through 76 artists each with 5 images, to its own perspective on contemporary illustration. Without ever taking themselves too seriously, they were able to share their viewpoints with those of the others.

The results are the illustrations you can enjoy by browsing through the following pages. They represent the best of what the jurors have been able to discover in the enormous pavilion/hangar. Happy viewing!

VALÉRIE CUSSAGUET after obtaining a degree in Law from Nanterre University and training in publishing at Paris XIII, Valérie Cussaguet began work in 1992 as a book promoter at Gallimard Jeunesse, subsequently moving to Bayard Éditions, again on the communications side of the business. In 1998, she helped set up Éditions Thierry Magnier, where for thirteen years she was involved with picture book publication. In 2013, with twenty years' publishing experience behind her, Valérie decided to start her own children's book publishing house, Les Fourmis Rouges. Today, with a catalogue of some ninety picture books, many of which have been translated into several languages, and numerous literary awards to its name, Les Fourmis Rouges is firmly established in the children's publishing scene. In 2016, Valérie also became an Associate Professor on the Master's Publishing Course at Clermont-Ferrand University.

ENRICO FORNAROLI is the Director of the Bologna's Fine Art Academy and also Chair of the Art Education and Teaching Department. For years he has been concerned with the mass media and children's literature. The curator of numerous imprints dedicated to comics, he acted as consultant for Panini Comics on the development of "I Classici del Fumetto" and "I Classici del Fumetto – Serie Oro" published by the Italian daily "La Repubblica." He has written many essays and catalogue overviews on comics, communication and cultural studies. Since 2006, Enrico has curated the Giornata Mafrica event "for popular literature" sponsored by the Natalino Sapegno Foundation.

LORENZO MATTOTTI studied Architecture at the University of Venice and started his career in the '70s as a comics writer. Often frequenting the stimulating scene of comics writers in Bologna, he founded, together with other artists, the magazine "Valvoline" (1983). The year after, he published his book *Fires*, a work that achieved international acclaim for his highly expressive and evocative style. Moving permanently to Paris in 1988, Lorenzo became part of the international illustration scene, exploring forms of artistic expression other than comics, although he continued to cultivate the genre. His many publications include *La zona fatua*, (released in 1998 by Albin Michel as part of a volume entitled *Murmure*), *L'Uomo alla Finestra* (Feltrinelli, 1992), *Le Voyage de Caboto* (Albin Michel, 1993), and *Stigmates*, first published in France in 1994 by Autrement in the anthology *Le Retour de Dieu* and further developed in *Le Bruit du Givre* (Seuil, 2003). Alongside his collaboration with newspapers like "The New Yorker," "Cosmopolitan," "Le Monde," "Süddeutsche Zeitung," "Il Corriere della Sera" and "La Repubblica," Lorenzo also accepted commissions from the visual communication sector, developing a particular interest in the language of film. In 2004, following his animation for children, *Eugenio e Pinocchio*, he created the illustrations for *Eros*, a film series directed by Michelangelo Antonioni, Steven Soderbergh and Wong Kar-wai. In 2008, he also collaborated on the collective animation Peur(s) du noir (2008). An animation project is yet again his more recent major focus: the feature film *The Bears Famous Invasion of Sicily*, produced by Prima Linea Productions and co-produced by Pathé, France 3 Cinéma and Indigo Film, winner of the Special Prize of the Gan Foundation for Cinema in 2016, and presented at the 2019 Cannes Film Festival.

CATHY OLMEDILLAS is the creative director and founder of Studio Anorak, the publisher of "Happy Mags for Kids, Anorak" and "DOT." In 2006, she launched the internationally acclaimed "Happy Mag for Kids, Anorak" when she couldn't find a fun, educational and collectable magazine to read with her son. Studio Anorak went on to launch a family-focused content agency producing pieces of communications for brands such as Airbnb, H&M and Pottermore, amongst others.

MACHIKO WAKATSUKI is the president and chief editor at Bronze Publishing Inc., based in Tokyo, Japan. Machiko was born in Kyoto and studied Aesthetics and Arts at Doshisha University. In 1983, she founded Bronze Publishing Inc., which, at the beginning, published mainly literal works and critical essays. Then in 1990, it published its first picture book for children entitled *Scribble Book Gomi Taro 50%* by Taro Gomi. This book is now translated into 18 different languages. Machiko's first visit to the Bologna Children's Book Fair in 1993 was an important eye-opening experience. She was dumbfounded by the variety of picture books published across the world and the efforts of the publishers who endeavor to make books for children by combining literature and art, using artistic expressions based firmly on local culture and history. From then on, she has frequented the Bologna Children's Book Fair every year for Bronze Publishing, which is now in its eighteenth year of attendance of the Fair. In 2016, Bronze Publishing was nominated as best Asian publisher for the "BOP – Bologna Prize for the Best Children's Publishers of the Year," and it received the Special Mention of the Fiction section of the BolognaRagazzi Award in 2017 for Shinsuke Yoshitake's *Still Stuck*.

2020 BOLOGNA ILLUSTRATORS EXHIBITION

PUBLISHER'S NOTE:

AS STATED IN THE EXHIBITION REGULATIONS,
EACH ILLUSTRATOR SUBMITTED TO THE JURY
A SEQUENCE OF FIVE IMAGES, WHICH IDEALLY
FORM A STORY. IN SOME CASES, WE DECIDED
TO REPRODUCE ONLY SOME OF THE ILLUS-
TRATIONS SO AS TO HIGHLIGHT THE STRENGTHS
THAT THE JURY SAW IN THE WORK OF EACH
ARTIST. BUT WE ALSO DECIDED TO MAIN-
TAIN THE ORIGINAL NUMBERS IN THE CAPTIONS
OF THE ILLUSTRATIONS THAT WERE PRESENTED.
WHERE NOT EXPLICITLY STATED OTHERWISE,
ILLUSTRATORS HAVE NOT BEEN PREVIOUSLY
PUBLISHED ELSEWHERE.

5

"COLUI CHE SONO." ILMIOLIBRO SELF PUBLISHING. 2016
"DOMANI VIENE DA IERI." FAUSTO LUPETTI EDITORE. BOLOGNA. 2015

FEDERICA AGLIETTI

BEHANCE.NET/EF94

Io e Giorgio Morandi (Autoritratto, 2018)
(Giorgio Morandi and I [Self-portrait, 2018])

Ink on paper • Fiction

Italy • *Bagno a Ripoli, 02 September 1994*

federicaaglietti@gmail.com • **0039 3311089658**

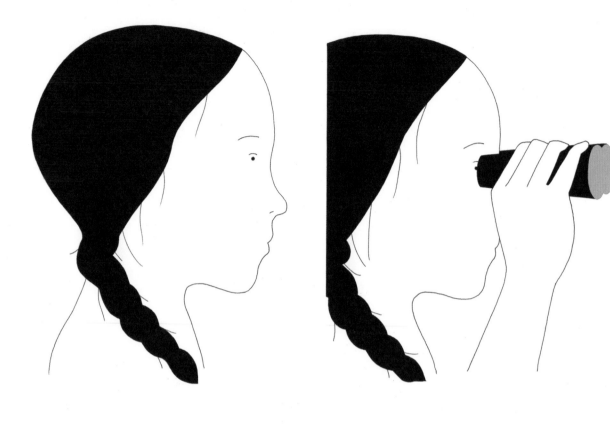

1 ALMA LIKES TO LOOK THROUGH HER WINDOWS. HER NEIGHBOURS AND THEIR LIVES
4 A FEW DAYS PASS BEFORE ALMA DARES TO LOOK AGAIN. WHEN SHE DOES. GHOSTS
ARE EVERYWHERE. NONCHALANTLY PLAYING PING PONG AROUND THE BUILDING

1

"SORTIE DE NUIT." BISCOTO ÉDITIONS. ANGOULÊME. TO BE PUBLISHED IN 2020
"LA RONDE DES SINGES." ALBIN MICHEL JEUNESSE. COLLECTION TRAPÈZE. PARIS. 2019
"L'IMAGIER DES DISPARUS." LE BARON PERCHÉ. PARIS. 2014

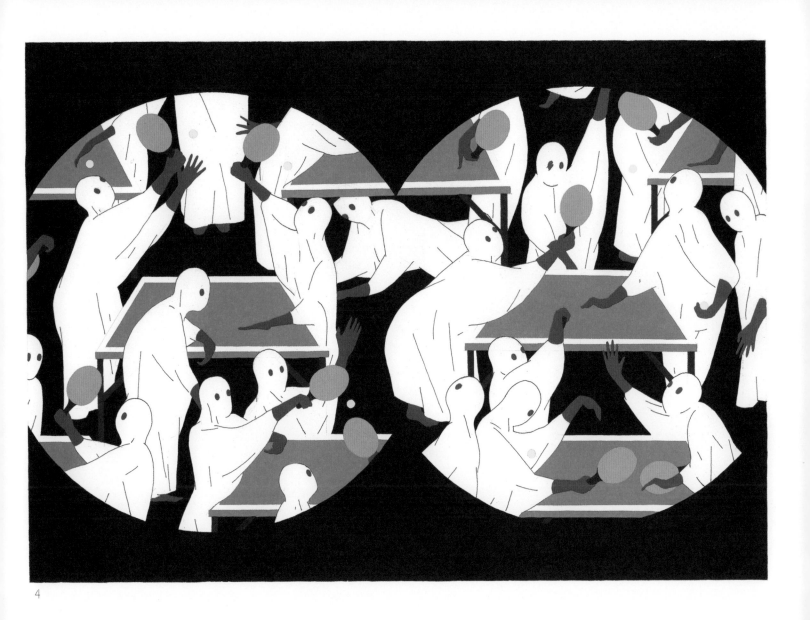

4

LAURIE AGUSTI
LAURIEAGUSTI.COM

L'immeuble d'à côté (Building next door) • Gouache, technical pen • Fiction
Albin Michel Jeunesse, Collection Trapèze, Paris, to be published, ISBN 2226449610

France • *Les Lilas, 24 January 1987*

lagusti@hotmail.fr • 0033 669906459

3

4

"UN QUADRATO / A SQUARE." CORRAINI EDIZIONI. MANTOVA. 2017
"UN MINUTO / ONE MINUTE." CORRAINI EDIZIONI. MANTOVA. 2016

5

3 A BOY WENT TO A PRIVATE EDUCATION INSTITUTE
4 A BOY WENT HOME AFTER THE CLASS
5 A BOY LIVES IN A SQUARE WORLD

SOMIN AHN

JADEINAPOND.COM

Square's Dream • Pencil, acrylic, digital media • Fiction
Changbi Publishers Inc., Gyeonggi-do, 2020, ISBN 9788936447571
Korea • *Seoul, 07 February 1981*

mojo81@naver.com • 0082 1068295808

3

AKIKOYA

AKIKOYA.WIXSITE.COM/AKIKOYA#

The Legends of Tōno

Marker pen, colored ink, calligraphy, Japanese brush-style pen • Fiction

Japan • *Fukushima, 26 November 1975*

yhirj784@yahoo.co.jp • 0081 08056800650

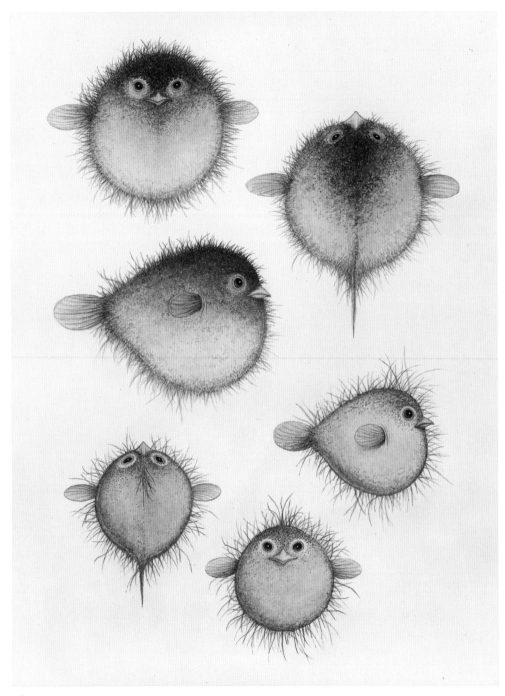

1

3

1 STRAWPUFFER FISH (TETRAODON ORBICULATUS)   3 LEAF RAY (PHASMANTICULA PLANARIA)

ALESSIO ALCINI

BEHANCE.NET/PAPEKKIO260761

Ultime scoperte nel mondo animale (Latest Discoveries in the Animal World)

Pencil and watercolor • Nonfiction

Italy • *Giulianova, 20 May 1993*

papecchio@gmail.com • 0039 3663897130

CYNTHIA ALONSO

CYNTHIA-ALONSO.COM

Inquieta / Many ways • Mixed media • Fiction

Savanna Books, Ribarroja, to be published

ISBN Castilian Spanish 9788494965470

ISBN Catalan 9788494965487

Argentina • *Buenos Aires, 26 July 1987*

hola@cynthia-alonso.com • 0049 17674351187

"RATÓN DE BIBLIOTECA / THE READER." PERIPLO EDICIONES. BUENOS AIRES. 2018
/ INTERLINK BOOKS. NORTHAMPTON. 2019
"UNDER THE CANOPY." FLYING EYE BOOKS. LONDON. 2018
"AQUÀRIO." ORFEU NEGRO. LISBOA. 2017 / CHRONICLE BOOKS. SAN FRANCISCO. 2018

1

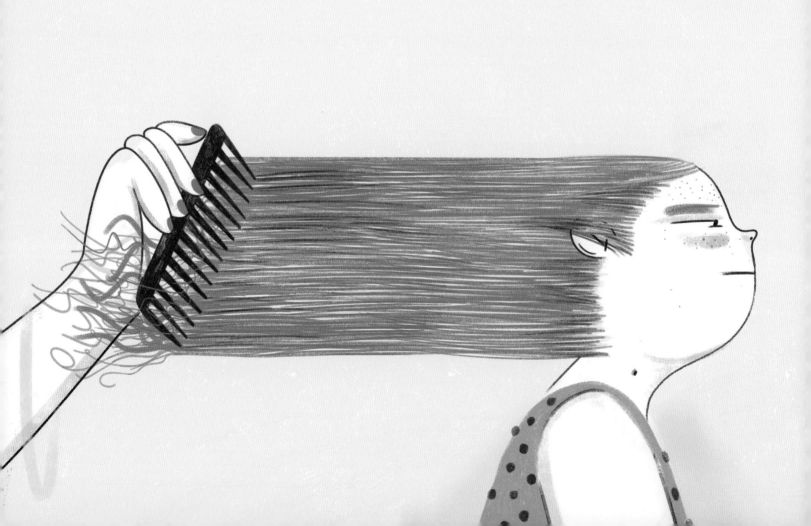

2

1

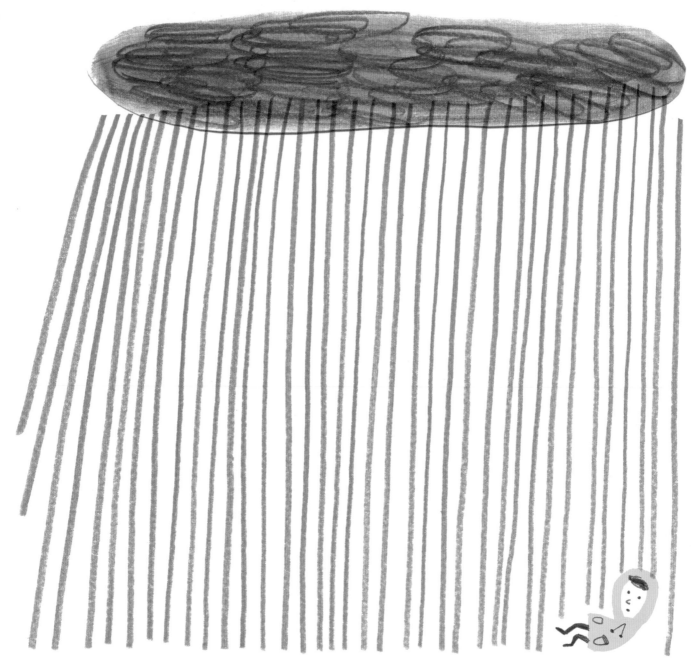

"SULLA VITA DEI LEMURI — BREVE TRATTATO DI STORIA NATURALE."
CORRAINI EDIZIONI. MANTOVA. 2020
"LA MIA SERA." EINAUDI RAGAZZI. SAN DORLIGO DELLA VALLE. 2020
"A CANÇÃO DO JARDINEIRO LOUCO." BRUAÁ. FIGUEIRA DA FOZ. 2019
"CONTAR." A BUEN PASO. BARCELONA. 2019
"PAROLA DI ASTRONAUTA." LAPIS EDIZIONI. ROMA. 2019
"ANIMALI IN CITTÀ." LAPIS EDIZIONI. ROMA. 2019
"L'ARRIVO DI SANTA LUCIA." CORRAINI EDIZIONI. MANTOVA. 2018
"STORIA DEL MEDITERRANEO IN 20 OGGETTI." EDITORI LATERZA. BARI. 2018
"ALTRI FILI INVISIBILI DELLA NATURA." LAPIS EDIZIONI. ROMA. 2018
"BLANCO COMO NIEVE / BLANC COM LA NEU." A BUEN PASO. BARCELONA. 2018
"IL NONNO BUGIARDO." CAMELOZAMPA. MONSELICE. 2018
"L'ENTRATA DI CRISTO A BRUXELLES / CHRIST'S ENTRY INTO BRUSSELS."
CORRAINI EDIZIONI. MANTOVA. 2017
"ELEFANTASY." LA NUOVA FRONTIERA EDITORE. ROMA. 2017
"PIANTE E ANIMALI TERRIBILI." LAPIS EDIZIONI. ROMA. 2017
"UN LIBRO SULLE BALENE / A BOOK ABOUT WHALES." CORRAINI EDIZIONI. MANTOVA. 2016
"LA ZUPPA DELL'ORCO." BIANCOENERO EDIZIONI. ROMA. 2016
"QUESTO È UN ALCE / IS THIS A MOOSE?." CORRAINI EDIZIONI. MANTOVA. 2015

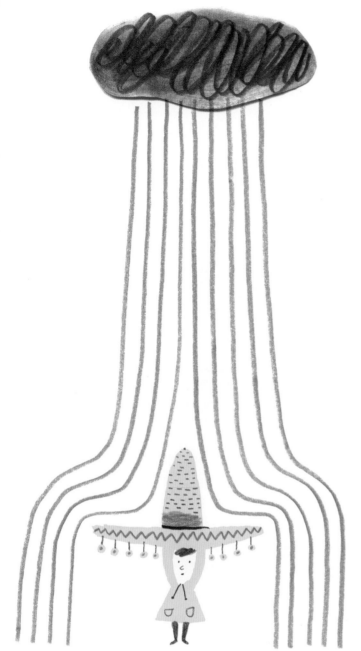
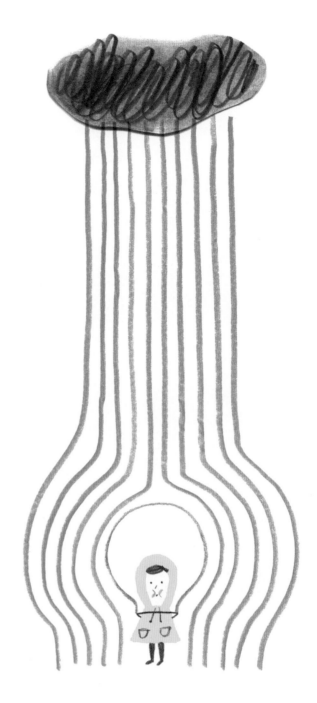

ANDREA ANTINORI
ANDREANTINORI.COM

The Great Battle • Mixed media • Fiction
Corraini Edizioni, Mantua, 2019, ISBN 9788875707675
Italy • *Recanati, 17 March 1992*
andreantinori1@gmail.com • 0039 3472391241

1

3

MICHAEL BARDEGGIA
BEHANCE.NET/BARDEGGIAMDB10

Il Meraviglioso Mago di Oz (The Wonderful Wizard of Oz)

Pantone felt pens, pen, colored pencils • Fiction

Arka Edizioni, Milan, 2019, ISBN 9788880722618

Italy • *Pesaro, 11 December 1993*

bardeggiamichael@gmail.com • **0039 3479993733**

3

2

4

2 GILGAMESH ON THE THRONE   3 IN THE CEDAR FOREST   4 ENKIDU AT THE TEMPLE OF ENLIL

MATTEO BERTON

MATTEOBERTON.COM

Gilgamesh et le secret de la vie-sans-fin (Gilgamesh and the Secret of Endless Life)

Digital media • Fiction

Amaterra, Lyon, 2018, ISBN 9782368561720

Italy • *Pisa, 25 September 1988*

matteberton@gmail.com • 0039 3465348238

1 MUSEUM

Chamuyo (Small Talk) • China ink, aniline • Fiction

Argentina • Buenos Aires, 13 June 1987

hola@joaquincamp.com.ar • 0034 698834519

JOAQUIN CAMP

JOAQUINCAMP.COM.AR

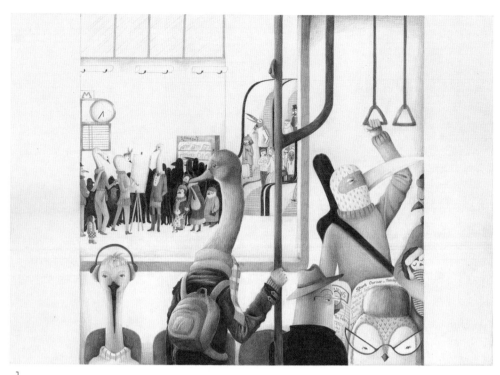

1

2

ACCADEMIA DI BELLE ARTI DI BOLOGNA
DIRECTOR: ENRICO FORNAROLI
COORDINATOR: OCTAVIA MONACO

3

5

ELISA CAVALIERE

The Ugly Duckling: a Modern Tale

Pencil • Fiction

Italy • *Bologna, 30 September 1997*

eli9709paint@gmail.com • 0039 3779112697

1

5

1 WHEN I WAS WAITING FOR MY MOM TO PICK ME UP. I SENT DOZENS OF EGGS TO MR. CAKE
2 WHEN I WAS WAITING FOR MY MOM TO PICK ME UP I STAYED ON A DESERT ISLAND FOR SEVEN WEEKS
5 WHEN I WAS WAITING FOR MY MOM TO PICK ME UP I HELPED THE DELIVERY MAN SEND THE PACKAGE ALONG ALLIGATOR AVENUE

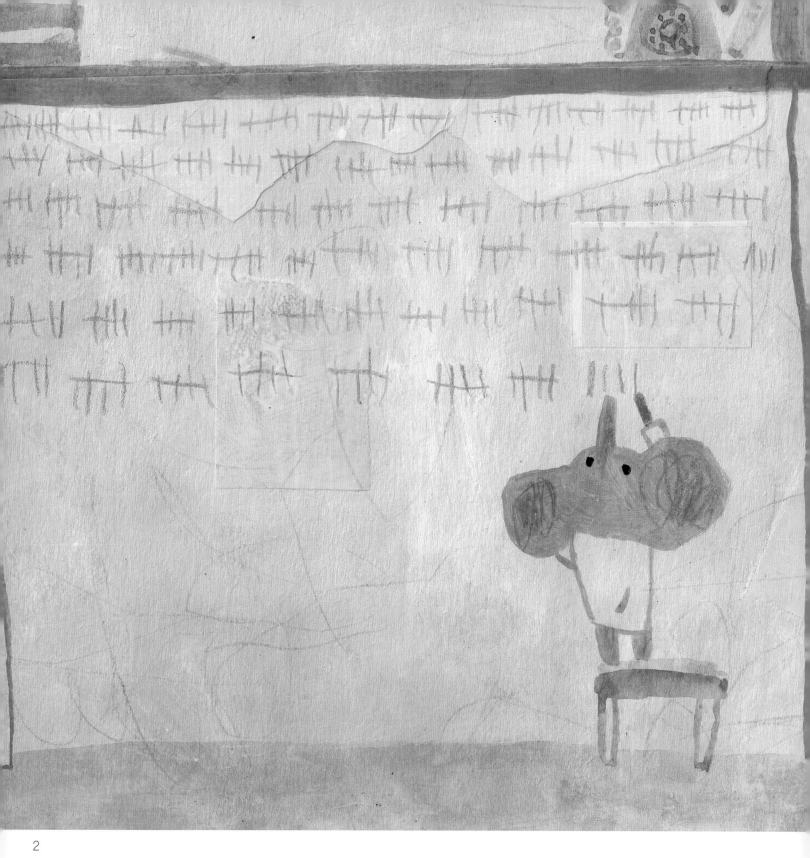

HSIAO-CHI CHANG

When I Was Waiting for My Mom to Pick Me Up After School

Mixed media • Fiction

The Eastern Publishing Co. Ltd, Taipei, to be published, ISBN 9789863383079

Taiwan • *Kaohsiung, 19 October 1986*

im.hsiaochi@gmail.com • 0088 626950381

2

3

 "HEY, YOU ARE GREAT TOO!" VISTA PUBLISHING, TAIPEI, 2019

4

5

2 WHAT FISHERMEN FISHED IS RUBBISH INSTEAD OF FISHES
3 MANUFACTURERS STILL MADE RUBBISH INTO CANNED FISH
4 SELLING THEM WITH ATTRACTIVE PACKAGING IN THE SUPERMARKET
5 PEOPLE STILL BOUGHT AND ATE THEM ELEGANTLY WITH KNIVES AND FORKS

CHIAO-YU CHEN

What Will Happen in the Future?

Digital media • Fiction

Taiwan • *Taipei, 30 August 1993*

yedda2079@gmail.com • 0088 60982368777

4

DANI CHOI
DANICHOI.COM

Private Rooms of Circus Sideshows Freaks

Mixed and digital media • Fiction

Korea • *Gangneung, 28 February 1994*

danichoiart@gmail.com • 0019178411754

JAM DONG

Ponds

Gouache, graphite, collage, digital media

Fiction

China • *Shanghai, 07 December 1990*

dongxingru1990@gmail.com • 0013305939166

"THE VOCAL TOUCHING BOOK (4 VOLUMES)."
XI'AN PUBLISHING HOUSE. XI'AN 2019

ANDRÉ DUCCI

ANDREDUCCI.ART.BR

O Livro da Selva (The Jungle Book)
Digital media • Fiction
Instituto Mojo de Comunicação Intercultural
São Paulo, 2018, ISBN 9788545510802
Italy • *Curitiba, 08 October 1977*
abducci@gmail.com • **0039 3515969287**

"GRANDE." POLVO. LISBOA. 2019
"FILM DO MUNDO." ARTE & LETRA.
CURITIBA. 2014
"TOCAR NA BANDA." ARTE & LETRA.
CURITIBA. 2010
"GUÍA DE RUAS SEM SAÍDA."
EDITH. SÃO PAULO. 2010

3

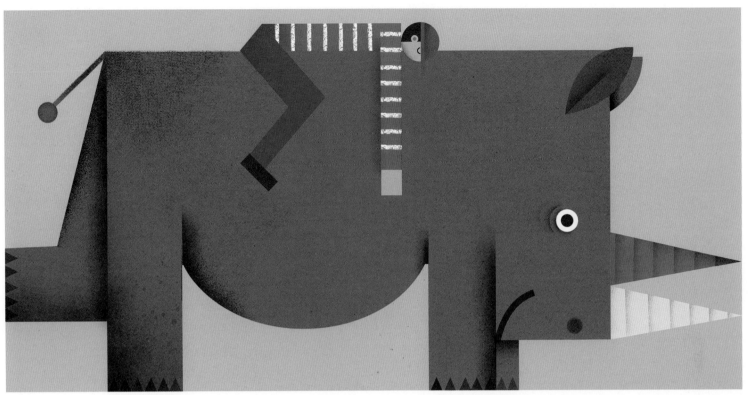

1

PHILIP GIORDANO
BEHANCE.NET/PHILIPGIORDANO

Same Planet Same Destiny, A Long Journey Together

Digital media • Fiction

Italy • *Savona, 15 January 1980*

sigur451@gmail.com • 0039 019991845

"I ATE SUNSHINE FOR BREAKFAST." FLYING EYE BOOKS. LONDON. 2020
"L'ÉTOILE DE ROBIN." EDITION MILAN. TOULOUSE. 2019
"D'ESTATE, D'INVERNO." TOPIPITTORI. MILANO. 2019
"LES SAISONS." EDITION MILAN. TOULOUSE. 2018
"GRATTACIELA." LA SPIGA. LORETO. 2017
"L'HIRONDELLE QUI VOULAIT VOIR L'HIVER." EDITION MILAN.
TOULOUSE. 2017
"LE PINGOUIN QUI AVAIT FROID." EDITION MILAN. TOULOUSE. 2016
"GALLITO PELÓN." OQO EDITORA. PONTEVEDRA. 2013
"LA PRINCESA NOCHE RESPLANDECIENTE." FUNDACIÓN SM. MADRID. 2011
"CHISSADOVE." ZOOLIBRI. REGGIO EMILIA. 2009

4

"CHANGEONS!." ÉDITIONS LA JOIE DE LIRE. GENÈVE. 2017
"50 KULISSEN 50 FILME." KNESEBECK VERLAG. MÜNCHEN. 2017
"100 FILM. LI RICONOSCERAI TUTTI." FRANCO COSIMO PANINI
EDITORE. MODENA. 2017
"DOUCE FRANCE - CES PAYSAGES QU'ON AIME."
ÉDITIONS MILAN - MILAN ET DEMI. TOULOUSE. 2016
"CENT FILMS: LES RECONNAÎTREZ-VOUS TOUS?."
ÉDITIONS MILAN - MILAN ET DEMI. TOULOUSE. 2016
"50 DÉCORS. 50 FILMS À DEVINER."
ÉDITIONS MILAN - MILAN ET DEMI. TOULOUSE. 2015
"LA FRANCE QUI GUEULE! PORTRAIT D'UNE FRANCE REBELLE."
ÉDITIONS MILAN - MILAN ET DEMI. TOULOUSE. 2015
"LA STORIA DI NABUCCO." EUM EDIZIONI UNIVERSITÀ
DI MACERATA. MACERATA. 2013

FRANCESCO GIUSTOZZI

BEHANCE.NET/FRANCESCOGIUSTOZZI

Hadrien e Napoleon e il libro delle avventure (Hadrien and Napoleon and the Book of Adventures)

Digital media • Fiction

Carthusia Edizioni, Milan, to be published

Italy • *Macerata, 18 May 1986*

francesco.giustozzi@hotmail.it • 0039 3331385337

1

ANGLIA RUSKIN UNIVERSITY - CAMBRIDGE SCHOOL OF ART
DIRECTOR: HARRIET RICHES.
COORDINATOR: SHELLEY ANN JACKSON

2

5

YAN HE

Brighton · Gouache, ink, pen, colored pencil, digital media · Nonfiction

China · *Beijing, 03 February 1995*

yan239960@gmail.com · 004407426969960

"THE ANCIENT WORLD IN 100 WORDS." QUATRO KNOWS. LONDON. 2019
"OSTINATO." PWM. KRAKÓW. 2019
"GLISSANDO." PWM. KRAKÓW. 2019
"ALIKWOTY." PWM. KRAKÓW. 2019
"KOLUMB. CAŁKIEM INNA HISTORIA." EGMONT. WARSZAW. 2019
"RAZ, DWA, TRZY, ZAŚNIJ TY!." ZNAK EMOTIKON. KRAKÓW. 2018
"O KOTACH." CZARNE. SĘKOWA. 2018
"L'ELEFANTE SULLA LUNA." MATILDA EDITRICE. FOGGIA. 2018
"WIERSZE DLA DZIECI." WARSTWY. WROCŁAW. 2017
"LODOROSTY I BLUSZCZARY." WOLNO. LUSOWO. 2017
"SŁOŃ NA KSIĘŻYCU." CENTRALA. POZNAN. 2016
"ELEPHANT ON THE MOON." CENTRALA. LONDON. 2016
"FERTILITY." CENTRALA. LONDON. 2015

Balonowa 5 (5 Bubblegum Street)
Colored pencils, digital media • Fiction
Egmont, Warsaw, 2019, ISBN 9788328144804

GOSIA HERBA

GOSIAHERBA.PL

Poland • Otawa, 17 February 1985

mail@gosiaherba.pl • 0048651446892

1

2

"LOS ESCRIBIDORES DE CARTAS." EDICIONES SM. MADRID. 2019

"MIGUE HACE UN LIBRO." MILRAZONES. SANTANDER. 2018

"LES AVENTURES D'UN RATOLÍ DE BIBLIOTECA." CRÜILLA. BARCELONA. 2018

"BARRIOS DE COLORES." MILRAZONES. SANTANDER. 2017

"FILOMENA FICALAPOTA." CRÜILLA. BARCELONA. 2017

"JASON Y LOS ARGONAUTAS." MILRAZONES. SANTANDER. 2016

"LA CAZADORA DE INDIANA JONES." EDICIONES SM. MADRID. 2016

"LLUEVE." EDICIONES SM. MADRID. 2016

"EL BAÑO DE CLEOPATRA." ANAYA. SALAMANCA. 2016

"COMO HACER TRABAJOS INCREIBLES CON INTERNET." ANAYA. SALAMANCA. 2015

"SAN JORGE Y EL DRAGON." JAGUAR. MADRID. 2014

"THE SELFISH GIANT." BUHOBOOKS. MADRID. 2012

3

4

KIKE IBÁÑEZ
KIKEIBANEZ.COM

Il segreto di Gino Bartali (The Secret of Gino Bartali)

Markers, colored pencils, digital media • Fiction

Spain • *Donosti, 06 September 1980*

kikeibanez@gmail.com • 0034 676831773

In your personal opinion, what qualities should an illustration absolutely have to be included in the selection of the Illustrators Exhibition?

I am always looking for new works that show the potential birth of a new picture book artist.

Picture book illustration has always expressed itself while receiving influences from various art forms such as printing, painting, picture book artists of the past, comics and animation.

The works we chose were mainly those with original styles, but in some we saw that those styles were still not sublimated into a personal and original approach. I believe, however, that these artists will eventually be able to reach that original form of expression through trial and error. If you want to be a picture book artist, you should continue to experiment persistently until you find your own style.

Engaging narrative, composition, design sense, originality, freshness, chromatic brilliance, monochromatic beauty . . . there are many things that are important for picture book illustration. But what is most important is the concept and message contained in the book. A book has a "background concept" as well as a "backbone." If the central concept does not act consistently as the backbone of a book, it cannot be conceived as such. So I chose illustrations in which I could perceive the book's concept in all five works.

How has the growing presence of digital techniques changed illustration?

Digital techniques have expanded the range of expression in illustration. Now you can draw directly on your computer, scan your drawings and add texture and color, do collages and create a work through many layers of editing. We see artists who have succeeded in producing illustrations of a kind never seen before by using this kind of mixed media approach.

But I do not think that these works can be immediately transformed into new picture books. These new media represent just one of the techniques available to the illustrator. A technique is useful only if you have a concept or a personal way of viewing the world.

We have seen many digital works during the selection process. What I would like illustrators to be especially careful about is the printing. If your works are made digitally, (in this competition) the works you have printed and submitted are regarded as the original work. If your works are printed on the wrong paper, they will not shine. Illustrators should also pay attention to color adjustment. Working with digital techniques also requires printing skills.

In the huge room where illustrations are displayed during the selection, they are arranged by country. Do differences still exist regarding styles, techniques and imaginaries in different geographical or cultural areas, or is illustration becoming increasingly global across the board?

While judging, I did not get the feeling that illustrations are becoming globally standardized. Picture books still have a very short history, of about 120 years. Beatrix Potter and Kate Greenaway were the pioneers. It is a book form that developed mainly in England, Europe and then in the United States. In many countries, picture books published in theses areas of origin have been taken as models. In the 20th century, many artists have experimented with new styles and those styles have produced mutual influences. I believe that the picture book has still not reached the point in which style, technique and ideas differ according to cultural and regional differences.

Picture books emerged when artists started to accompany folktales or poems with images. In Japan, these publications started about a century ago, but the *Sosaku Ehon*, picture books devised with the original ideas of artists, started to appear in the 1960s and 1970s. Also in Korea, picture book artists started to emerge very recently, after the year 2000.

There are many countries in which original picture books are still not published. If the unique styles, techniques and ideas of these regional cultures would be projected into publications, the world of picture books will become more diverse. For example, take a look at the wonderful picture books published by India's Tara Books, made with their own printing and binding techniques. They have been able to elevate traditional styles into new forms of expression. New picture book artists will emerge very soon from China as well. I believe that in Asia, it is possible to establish a new kind of "culture" of the picture book.

Emigration has also brought about second-generation artists with fresh styles who have parents from different cultural backgrounds. The mixture of cultures will open up new horizons for the picture book.

Can children's books and children's illustration tackle social subjects, such as war, loss and poverty? Or should children be protected from these topics, as they won't be able to fully understand them?

As a publisher, I would like to tackle social themes. Our readers are aged 0 to 120. The picture book is a medium of expression where art and literature meet, but I would like to focus on making books that can be read from when you are very young. Until now we have published: Tomi Ungerer's *Die Blaue Wolke*, Jimmy Liao's *Under the Same Moon*, Yoshifumi Hasegawa's *Peace is Wonderful*, and Shuntarō Tanikawa's *Peace and War*.

On television and the web, children are exposed every day to war, famine, poverty, bereavement and environmental issues in the world. I think they are sensing how in this global society those problems are actually related to their everyday lives. How can we represent these problems with clarity so that children can understand them, without being too serious, and by focusing on the essence?

This is exactly where the ability of the artist and the editor will be challenged. How will children interpret and understand these unavoidable social problems in their lives? I would like my picture books to grasp these problems with hope and express the courage to overcome them.

In this edition, there were some entries that dealt with social themes, but I thought there should have been more.

What are the qualities that in your view an illustration should have to be included in the selection of the Illustrators Exhibition?

First of all, the ability to capture the gaze of the observer. To attract viewers in the engaging experience of the narration. It should also be a mixture of original style, technical ability, compositional solidity, rhythm, balance. Above all, it should have the capacity to sum up the universe of its maker.

Are there still spaces for experimentation in the field of illustration and in illustrated books for children? If so, what are they?

Without the possibility of experimenting we would be left only with reworking of familiar things, mannerism as an end in itself; instead, I think the margins for exploration of new expressive territories in illustration are still very vast. For example, in the sharing of different visual cultures apparently standardized by the market, or in the ability to cross languages and contaminate techniques. But to do this, one has to train the gaze and know the history (of illustration).

Looking at the submitted works, have you been able to identify trends or fashions that tend to repeat themselves? Should fashions always be rejected, or are they also a legitimate reflection of the spirit of the times?

Fortunately, the variety of styles and the diversity of approaches to the image demonstrate that in spite of being in a globalized, interconnected dimension, the differences can prevail over standardization, and the factors of originality and innovation over fashions and the temptation to indulge in repetition.

"HAÏKUS DE SIBÉRIE." ÉDITIONS SARBACANE. PARIS. 2019.
"SIBIRO HAIKU." AUKSO ŽUVYS. VILNIUS. 2017

LINA ITAGAKI
LINAITAGAKI.COM

Vilniaus rūmai ir jų šeimininkai (Vilnius Palace and its Lords)
Colored pencils, digital media • Nonfiction
Tikra Knyga, Vilnius, 2019, ISBN 9786098142549
Lithuania • Kaunas, 30 September 1979
linaitagaki@gmail.com • 0037 069926167

4 TRIUMPHAL PROCESSION

2

3

PICTURE BOOK IMAGINATION
DIRECTOR: SANGHYUN CHUN
COORDINATOR: JEONGWON LEE

74

BORA JIN

Breathe in, Breathe out
Dry point, acrylic, pencil, colored
pencil, marker, digital media • Fiction
Woongjin Think Big Co. Ltd, Paju-si,
to be published
Korea • *Seoul, 08 November 1990*
boraborajin@gmail.com • 0082 1089834763

1

2

SI PICTURE BOOK SCHOOL
DIRECTOR/COORDINATOR: SUNKYUNG CHO

4

5

1 A SHIP ARRIVED AT DAWN AT THE PIER AFTER FISHING ALL NIGHT IN THE SEA   5 THE AUCTION BEGINS

2 THE CAPTURED FISH ARE LOWERED FROM THE BOAT   4 BUYERS BID ON THE FISH

KAWON KIM

Dawn Market

Gouache, oil-pastel, pencil • Nonfiction

Korea • *Seoul, 20 March 1977*

lamic003@naver.com • 0082 1057797732

1

HAW - HAMBURG UNIVERSITY OF APPLIED SCIENCES
DIRECTOR: MICHA TEUSCHER
COORDINATOR: BERND MÖLCK-TASSEL

2

3

4

5

1 EARLY 19TH CENTURY   2 SPRING. SUNNY   3 SUMMER. RAIN   4 FALL. SUNSET   5 HALLOWEEN. NIGHT

1 FLY 4 FLEA

MIHWA KIM

A Bench Story
Digital media • Fiction
Korea • *Daejeon, 07 August 1985*
mihakim@gmx.de • 0049 15787797827

1

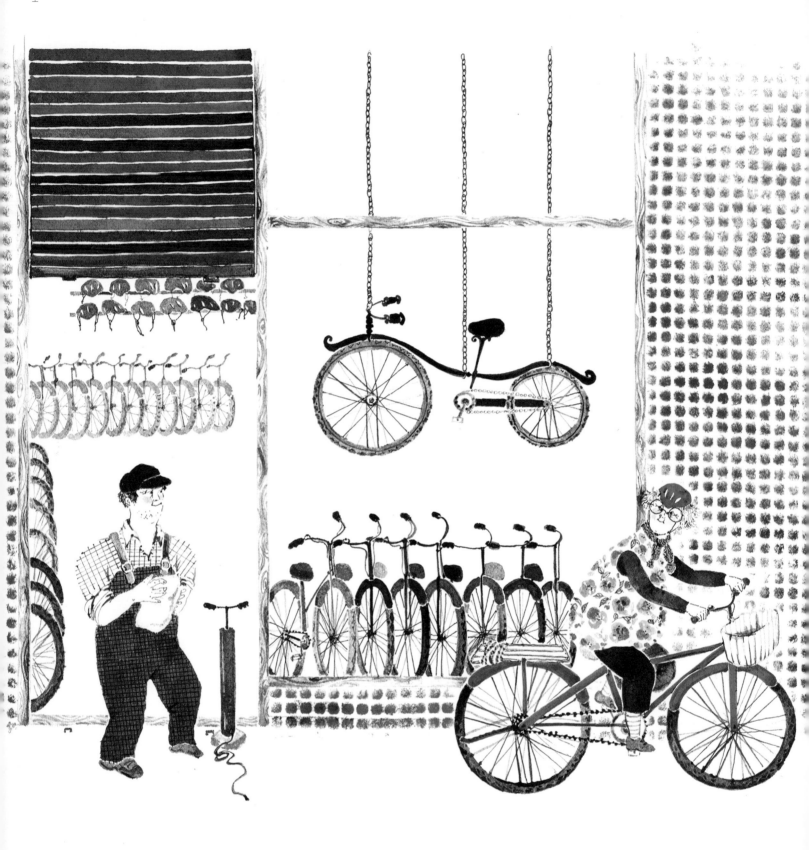

PICTURE BOOK HYANG INSTITUTE
DIRECTOR: KIM HYANG-SU

YUKYUNG KIM

Miss Tinkle, Where Are You Going?
Colored ink, acrylic • Fiction
Seedbook, Seoul, 2019, ISBN 9791160512694(77810)
Korea • *Seoul, 08 November 1970*
ggamsiii@hanmail.net • 00821089219179

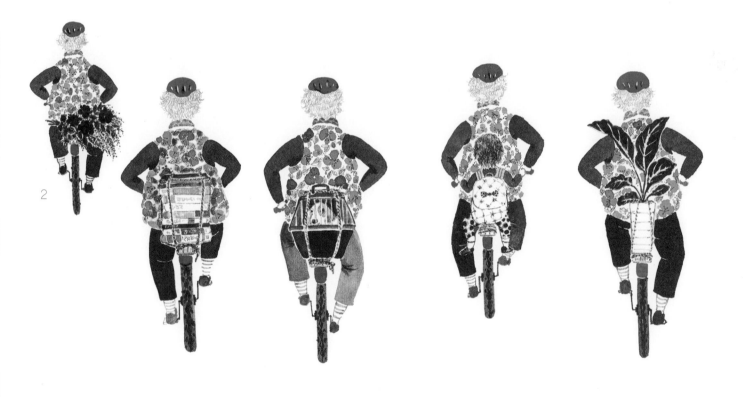

2

1 SHE FILLS THE BIKE'S TIRES WITH AIR AND RIDES OFF TO SOMEWHERE. "WHERE ARE YOU GOING?" 2 SHE HELPS HER NEIGHBORS. RIDING HER BIKE

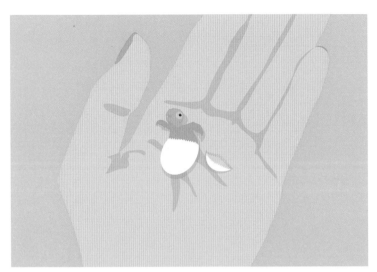

2

3

4

5

2 HELLO! THE WORLD   3 EAT! EAT! EAT!   5 THE LITTLE BIRD HAS GROWN INTO A DINOSAUR

4 THE LITTLE BIRD CAN EAT BY HERSELF

KOICHI KONATSU
KOICHIKONATSU.COM

My Cute Little Bird
Digital media • Fiction
No Bird No Life, Osaka, to be published, ISBN 9784908683220

Japan • *Osaka, 17 February 1974*

koichi.konatsu@me.com • 0081 9010226588

1

2

5

MENG-HSUAN KUAN
FACEBOOK.COM/TATAMIKUAN

A Little Trip
Drypoint, chine-collé, acrylic,
pencil • Fiction
Taiwan • *Kaohsiung City*
11 July 1982
tatami_7711@hotmail.com
0088 6958778911

1

"TA MAŁPA POSZŁA DO NIEBA." WYDAWNICTWO KOMIKSOWE. WARSZAW. 2018
"CHORE HISTORIE." KOCUR BURY. WARSZAW. 2017
"GŁOŚNE ZNIKNIĘCIE." KOCUR BURY. WARSZAW. 2016

5

GOSIA KULIK
GOSIAKULIK.COM

Jak ugryzc teatr wspolczesny? (How to Figure Out the Contemporary Theater?)

Pencil, digital media • Nonfiction

Fundacja na Rzecz Kultury i Edukacji im. Tymoteusza Karpowicza,

Wrocław, 2019, ISBN 9788394958381

Poland • *Piekary Śląskie, 15 July 1985*

gosiakulik.ilustrator@gmail.com • 0048 506848619

88

2

"LITTLE BIG TRAM." COTTON TREE PUBLISHING LTD.
HONG KONG. 2017

ANGLIA RUSKIN UNIVERSITY - CAMBRIDGE SCHOOL OF ART
DIRECTOR: HARRIET RICHES
COORDINATOR: SHELLEY ANN JACKSON

KIN CHOI LAM
LAMKINCHOI.COM

Dreaming • Monoprint, digital media • Fiction
Hong Kong, China • *Guangdong, 26 April 1988*
kinclam8@gmail.com • 0044 7490868340

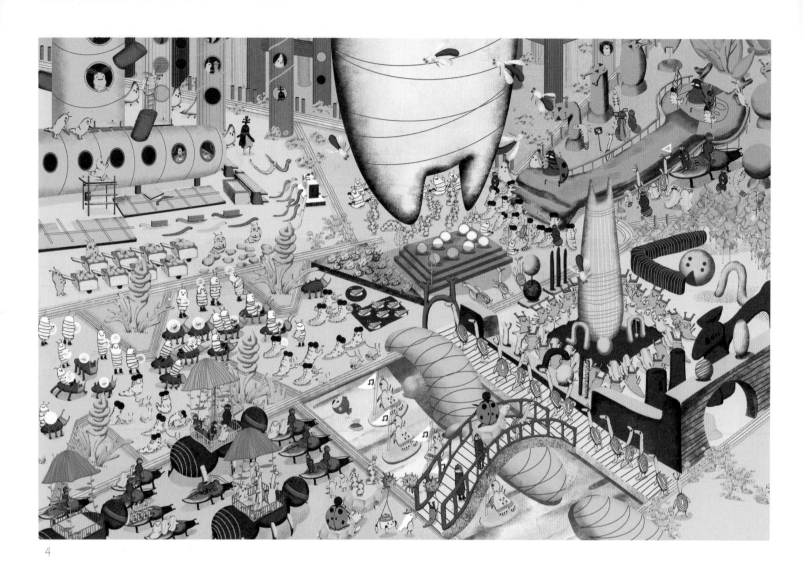

4

PICTURE BOOK HYANG INSTITUTE
DIRECTOR/COORDINATOR: KIM HYANG-SU

5

JIEUN LEE

The Great Apaturaillia • Digital media • Fiction

Gloyeon, Seoul, 2019, ISBN 9788992704670

Korea • *Seoul, 22 November 1991*

bigeye1122@naver.com • 0082 1091874239

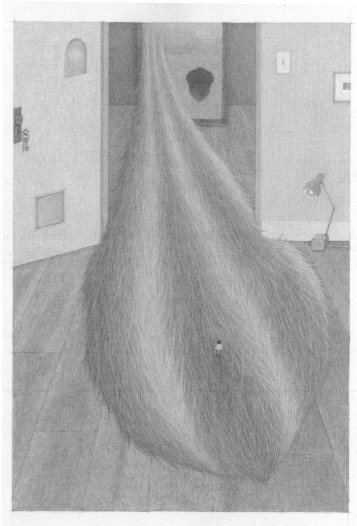

1

2

4

5

1 BEYOND THE RAUCOUS FIELDS   2 THE SHRUNKEN MAN ENTERS THE PICTURE FRAME OF A SQUIRREL
4 IN THE ACORN. HE LOOKS AT A HORSE OUTSIDE THE WINDOW   5 THE HORSE LOOKS AT HIM IN THE ACORN

JINHEE LEE

LEEJINHEE.COM

The Acorn Time • Mixed media • Fiction

Gloyeon, Seoul, 2019, ISBN 9788992704663 77810

Korea • *Seoul, 23 May 1983*

duetbook@naver.com • 0082 1077027033

2

1 ONE DAY. BAU AND JIN SAW A STRANGE RED BUTTERFLY FLYING INTO THEIR ROOM

2 THAT NIGHT. MY FAMILY FELL INTO A SWEET SLEEP. PUPPY BAU ALSO FELL ASLEEP. I WAS JUST FALLING ASLEEP

JINHWA LEE

Shrunkham_Blanccum
Gouache, pencil, digital media • Fiction
Korea • *Seoul, 11 May 1972*
zenastar@naver.com • 0082 1030517881

1

2

SI PICTURE BOOK SCHOOL
DIRECTOR/COORDINATOR: SUNKYUNG CHO

3

4

1 SURFERS WAIT FOR WAVES IN THE SEA   2 AS SURFERS COMPETE WITH EACH OTHER TO RIDE THE WAVE.
THEIR WILD NATURE IS AWOKEN AND THEY BECOME ANIMALS   3 WHILE THE SURFERS WERE FIGHTING.
A HUGE WAVE HIT THEM   4 SURFERS FELL OFF THEIR BOARDS AND THRASHED WILDLY IN THE WATER

MOONYO LEE
MOONYOLEE.COM

Surf • Digital media, risography • Fiction

Korea • *Daejeon, 22 September 1987*

moonyo.book@gmail.com • 0082 1092337710

1

2

NICOLAS LIGUORI

La vache aquatique, d'après une nouvelle de Nicola Lisi
(The Water Cow, from a story by Nicola Lisi)
Alexeïeff-Parker pinscreen of the CNC – Centre National du Cinéma et de l'image animée • Fiction

France • *Lille, 29 July 1981*

nicolas.liguori9@gmail.com • 0033 667050613

2

3

4

5

2 (SCRATCHING) BUZZING ... 3 BANG! ... 4 (SILENCE)... (BUZZING) ... 5 .... BUZZING...

CHIEN-YU LIN
INSTAGRAM.COM/CY___MA/

A Biting Game

Gouache, ink, mineral pigment • Fiction

Taiwan • *Taipei 3 September 1997*

chienyu1862@gmail.com • 00886937810595

In your personal opinion, which qualities must an illustration absolutely have to be included in the selection of the Illustrators Exhibition?

The criterias I used for the selection are the same I use when I commission work for our magazines: that balance between a charming and unique idea that captures what childhood is about and a visual treatment that suits the story well. It is often hard to put into words as this is so instinctive in my case, but I was looking for a special combination of an imaginative story mixed with how it is conveyed on an emotional and technical level. I wanted to be drawn into a world and wow'ed by the craft that went into creating that world.

Today, illustrated books are competing for children's time and attention with many digital forms of entertainment. Is it harder nowadays to capture the attention of a child with a traditional means like a picture book than it was in the past?

I think books and the printed matter generally will always have a huge place in children's lives. It is true that kids spend more time online than they did 30 years ago, but they also spend less time outdoors than they did in the past so maybe the time they spend online is the time they used to spend playing outside. Because as far as I have read, children's books sales (in the UK anyway) are on the up, so this means to me that actually, parents are aware of the pitfalls of too much screen culture and they favor print instead.

Is a good illustrator always a good illustrator of children's books?

The short answer is yes, provided they connect with wonder, imagination and their inner child.

This question reminds me of the criticism we received when we first launched "Anorak Magazine," as some industry people would say that, visually, it was too "sophisticated" for kids and clearly not aimed at them! They were sort of correct, as 90% of the artists we commissioned when we first started 13 years ago had never done anything for children. However, it didn't mean that they couldn't do anything for kids, it's just they'd never been given the opportunity.

Our view has always been that children are a lot more sophisticated than we give them credit for and we have always championed giving children and parents a choice in terms of aesthetic so they don't live in a dull homogenized world.

In your view, what are the qualities an illustration should have in order to be included in the selection for the Illustrators Exhibition?

Professionalism, culture, a profound personal poetic. Knowledge of the present illustration scene. Knowledge of art history and artistic languages in general. Technical ability. Awareness of its educational role. Courage.

How important is it for an illustrator to be "original?"

I think it is important not to seek an original and different graphic formula, but to have a versatile, erudite, strong, sensitive and courageous personality. Only in this way can the result be a unique, singular image.

With respect to those who perform other roles in the world of publishing, does an illustrator have more tools with which to judge the work of another illustrator? Or is there the risk of judging things through the filter of one's own work?

The illustrator can better understand certain mechanisms of the creation of an image, for a deeper assessment of the richness or shortcomings of the drawing, from a technical standpoint . . . the risk is always there, even when the person doing the judging is a publisher or an editor. You have to take different perspectives into account. One of the most important and difficult things for an illustrator is to have a detached view of the work; to know how to judge with another eye (the third one).

In your view, what are the qualities an illustration should have to enter the selection for the Illustrators Exhibition?

The members of the jury were not necessarily attracted by the same images and did not have the same expectations. The jury's choice is not the sum of personal tastes, but the result of collective thinking about what this exhibition should represent for professionals, publishers or illustrators. After a short time, the desire to present a wide range of styles and trends got the upper hand. The style with which the illustrator identifies is not so important. What is essential is that the image should have force and originality to stand out amidst hundreds of other illustrations.

Should a good illustrator have a recognizable style, or is there the risk of falling into a sort of self-plagiarism?

This is a complex question that gets to the heart of the work of an artist. I would tend to say yes, I think it is essential for an illustrator to have a recognizable style. As a publisher, I am attracted by strong personal imagery. When an artist is young, he or she often goes through a period of formation, absorbing different influences before finding a personal style. The artist's task, at times with the help of teachers and/or editors, is to trace a specific path in search of their own style. Afterwards, the situation is reversed. As you grow, you have to stay free and to experiment, keeping faith with your own path. It is a delicate balance, but necessary if you want to "last." I think it is possible only by continuing to work in a personal way, free from any commercial or imposed requirements.

Examining the submitted works, did you find recurring themes? Were there themes you were hoping to find, but didn't?

I imagined there would have been a strong presence of the fundamental issues of our society, though they have been widely addressed on the children's book market (feminism, sexual and gender identities, vegan diet, positive education, personal growth, meditation), but that was not the case. The themes varied, as did the styles.

I was surprised, however, by the rather secondary role assigned to humor in the submitted works. Usually it is in the foreground in children's literature.

A publisher can be seen as an intermediary between the creativity and work of artists and the demands of the market. Is it hard to reconcile these two levels?

I think it depends on the economic return you expect from the publication, and the time we are willing to grant to a book in order to turn a profit . . . If the return has to be immediate and sufficient to cover not only the work behind the book but also dividends for investors, it is hard—if not impossible—to reconcile creativity and market demand.

But if the financial expectations remain modest, this connection between the market and creativity will be the central focus of the work of the editor, which is exactly why this job is so exciting. To take the risk of investing in creativity puts you in a dangerous position, of course, but it is a matter of choosing to give a strong identity to the publishing house. And this, in my view, is a way to ensure longevity.

1

2

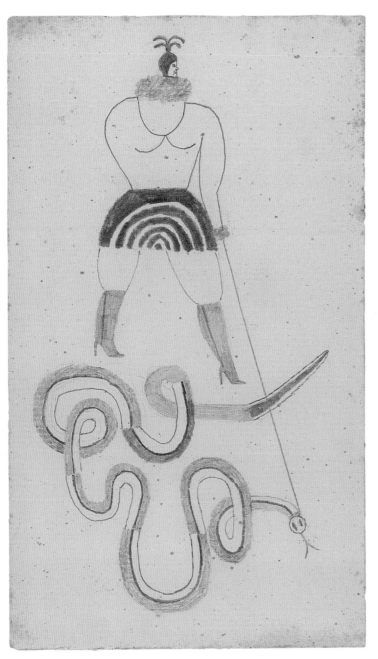

4

5

MARTA LONARDI
MARTALONARDI.IT

Interaction Design

Pencil on paper • Fiction

Italy • *Mantua, 17 August 1993*

info@martalonardi.it • 0039 3316219833

JEAN MALLARD

JEANMALLARD.TUMBLR.COM

Corsa degli animali (da un testo di Daniil Charms)
(The Animal Race [from a text by Daniil Kharms])
Watercolor, gouache, pencils, digital media • Fiction
Camelozampa, Monselice, to be published
France • *Paris, 02 June 1997*
jemableu@gmail.com • 0033 768335662

ARS IN FABULA - MASTER IN ILLUSTRATION FOR PUBLISHING
DIRECTOR: MAURO EVANGELISTA
COORDINATOR: ALESSANDRA SCONOSCIUTO

2

5

PHOOLAN MATZAK

Homeless • Woodcut • Nonfiction
Germany • *Lüneburg, 23 January 1995*
phoolan@live.de • **0049 015788091058**

1   2

"MINA'S DIARY." EDITION DELCOURT. PARIS (TO BE PUBLISHED)
"CHANBARA." SERGIO BONELLI EDITORE. MILANO. 2020
"REBECCA DEI RAGNI." IL CASTORO EDIZIONI. MILANO. 2019
"THE STORY THAT CANNOT BE TOLD." SIMON & SCHUSTER. NEW YORK. 2019
"BEYOND THE DOORS." PENGUIN RANDOM HOUSE. LONDON. 2017
"MON AME MON AMOUR. LES PLUS BELLES HISTOIRES D'AMOUR."
MILAN JEUNESSE. TOULOUSE. 2017
"SHOTARO." MONDADORI. SEGRATE. 2017
"THE ATLAS OF IMAGINARY PLACES." MONDADORI. SEGRATE. 2017
"THE WELL AT THE WORLD'S END." OXFORD UNIVERSITY PRESS. OXFORD. 2016
"THE BONE SNATCHER." PENGUIN RANDOM HOUSE. LONDON. 2016
"HORUS AND THE CURSE OF EVERLASTING REGRET." PENGUIN RANDOM HOUSE. LONDON. 2015
"OSSIAN E GRACE." MONDADORI. SEGRATE. 2015
"ROMEO AND JULIET." OXFORD UNIVERSITY PRESS. OXFORD. 2015
"BONS BAISERS RATES DE VENISE." GULFSTREAM EDITEUR. NANTES. 2014
"CARMILLA." EDITION SOLEIL. PARIS. 2014
"IL GIARDINO SEGRETO." LA SPIGA EDIZIONI. LORETO. 2012

3

4

ISABELLA MAZZANTI
INSTAGRAM.COM/ISUNIJA

Haikyo • Colored pencils, ink • Fiction

Italy • *Velletri, 08 March 1982*

isabella.mazzanti@gmail.com • 0039 3931809087

2

NAIDA MAZZENGA

NAIDAMAZZENGA.CARGO.SITE

**Tutto quello che faccio quando non ho voglia di disegnare
(All the Things I Do When I Don't Feel Like Drawing)**

Digital media, Risograph printing • Fiction

Italy • *Sora, 26 August 1991*

naida.mazzenga2@gmail.com • 0039 3496920986, 0034 632564423

1 FIRST CONTACT. CASOULI THE CAT GETS CAUGHT BY AN ILLEGAL TRAP FOR ANIMALS. THIS STARTS A COOPERATION WITH WILD ANIMALS AND HUMANS. IN AIM TO STOP THE ILLEGAL ACTIVITY IN THE FOREST.
3 WORKING TOGETHER. THE ANIMALS OF THE FOREST HAVE FOUND THE HIDING PLACE OF THE HUNTERS AND CARRY OUT A WELL PLANNED ATTACK TO CAPTURE THEM FOR A POLICE TO FIND THEM
4 THE ANIMAL REFUGE FOREST. CASOULI THE CAT IS BEING WELCOMED TO THE REFUGE FOREST WHERE ALL THE ANIMALS LIVE PEACEFULLY TOGETHER. HE IS NOW A FULL MEMBER OF THE SECRET PLACE
5 CHRISTMAS FOR THE ANIMALS. GRANDPA AND GRANDMA SERVE FOOD FOR ALL THE ANIMALS IN A BARN TO THANK THEM. THERE WAS HAY. CARROTS. NUTS. BERRIES. MEAT AND TURNIPS: SOMETHING FOR EVERYBODY

1

3

118

4

5

PINJA MERETOJA
PINJAMERETOJA.COM

Kissa Kasuli ja eläintent turvametsä
(Casouli the Cat and the Animal Refuge Forest)

Digital media • Fiction

Aviador Kustannus, Rajamäki, 2019, ISBN 9789527063781

Finland • *Turku, 20 July 1982*

pinja@pinjameretoja.com • 0035 8405559885

"POP POP GARDEN BALSAM." BEAR BOOKS INC., SEOUL, 2019
"CLOUD FLOWERS." JEI CORPORATION, SEOUL, 2018
"HUSH." JEI CORPORATION, SEOUL, 2017
"CHERRY." FATATRAC, BOLOGNA, 2017

3

2

2 LUCY IS EXCITED AND RUSHES AWAY AHEAD OF ME   3 WE MEET A ROAD FULL OF DAISIES
5 I ALSO HEAR THE SOUND OF FROGS AMONG WILLOW LEAVES. RIBBIT. RIBBIT. RIBBIT....

MYUNG-YE MOON

On Summer Nights

Digital media • Fiction

JEI Corporation, Seoul, 2019, ISBN 9788974993702

Korea • *Seoul, 10 April 1975*

mmun13@hanmail.net • 0082 1099655567

1

3

"A CIDADE DOS ANIMAIS." ORFEU NEGRO. LISBOA. 2017
"HAY CLASES SOCIALES." MEDIA VACA. VALENCIA. 2014

4

5

JOAN NEGRESCOLOR

NEGRESCOLOR.COM

Eu, Alfonsina (I, Alfonsina) • Digital media • Nonfiction

Orfeu Negro, Lisbon, 2019, ISBN 9789898868510

Spain • *Barcelona, 16 May 1978*

negrescolor@gmail.com • 0034 636898603

1

2

3

4

PICTURE BOOK HYANG INSTITUTE
DIRECTOR/COORDINATOR: KIM HYANG-SU

5

SE NA OH

Iceberg • Digital media • Fiction
Bandal Publishing, Paju, Gyeonggi-do, 2019, ISBN 97889816477810
Korea • *Jeon-ju, 15 August 1975*
art534@hanmail.net • 0082 1099830739

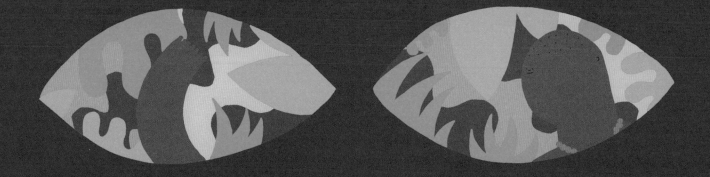

1

3

TOMÁS OLIVOS
TOMASOLIVOS.COM

El gran espíritu (The Great Spirit) · Digital media · Fiction

Saposcat Editorial, Santiago de Chile, 2019, ISBN 9789569866111

Chile · *Santiago, 06 August 1987*

tomas.olivos@gmail.com · 0034 695273765

5

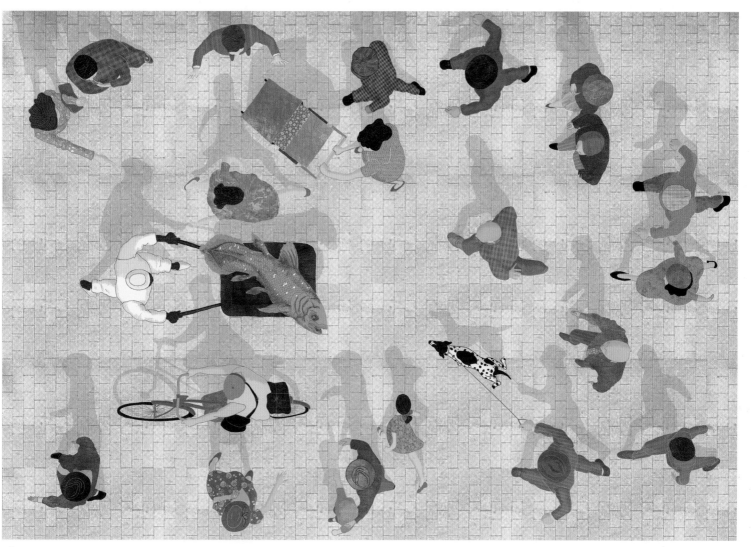

2

BERTA PARAMO
BERTAPARAMO.COM

The Charm of Coelacanth
Digital media • Nonfiction
Spain • *Burgos, 31 December 1975*
b.paramo@gmail.com • 0034 667900472

ARS IN FABULA - MASTER IN ILLUSTRATION FOR PUBLISHING
DIRECTOR: MAURO EVANGELISTA
COORDINATOR: ALESSANDRA SCONOSCIUTO

GIULIA PARODI

Le Tendine di Tata Lugton (The Curtains of Nanny Lugton)

Watercolor, colored pencils • Fiction

Italy • *Genoa, 29 September 1987*

giulia.parodi@hotmail.it • 0039 3425825048

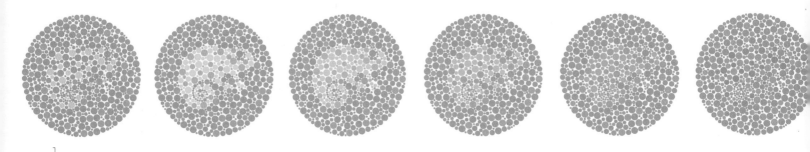

1

ÉCOLE ESTIENNE - ÉCOLE SUPÉRIEURE DES ARTS ET INDUSTRIES GRAPHIQUES
DIRECTOR: ANNIE-CLAUDE RUESCAS
COORDINATOR: MATTHIEU LAMBERT

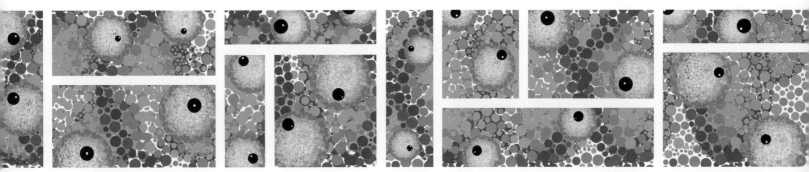

AMBRE RENAULT-FAIVRE D'ARCIER

Chameleon • Mixed media • Nonfiction

France • *Montpellier, 29 September 1998*

ambrerenault@orange.fr • 0033 0631610927

1

2

134

5

ELENA REPETUR

BEHANCE.NET/REPETUR

INSTAGRAM.COM/REPETULENKA

Odyssey Is Looking for a Friend

Pencil, watercolor • Fiction

Children's Literature, Moscow, 2020, ISBN 9785080062254

Russia • *Kokshetau, 18 February 1979*

marmarta@yandex.ru • 0079 096645761

2

4

ANGLIA RUSKIN UNIVERSITY - CAMBRIDGE SCHOOL OF ART
DIRECTOR: HARRIET RICHES
COORDINATOR: SHELLEY ANN JACKSON

1

1 WHO MIGHT HAVE FOUND MY LOST PENCIL CASE? 2 WAS IT THE GUY WITH THAT BIG MOUSTACHE? 4 OR WAS IT THE OLDER GENTLEMAN?

ROOZEBOOS

ROOZEBOOS.COM

A Case of Pencil People

Risograph · Fiction

Netherlands · *Arnhem, 13 December 1994*

annerooskleiss@gmail.com · 0031 648966956

1

"WÄR ICH PIRAT..." PETER HAMMER VERLAG. WUPPERTAL. 2012
"AM LIEBSTEN EINE KATZE." PETER HAMMER VERLAG. WUPPERTAL. 2010
"MIA MIT DEM HUT." PETER HAMMER VERLAG. WUPPERTAL. 2007
"EMIL WIRD SIEBEN." PETER HAMMER VERLAG. WUPPERTAL. 2005
"KANNST DU BRÜLLEN." PETER HAMMER VERLAG. WUPPERTAL. 2003

2

ANDRÉ RÖSLER
DER-ROESLER.DE

On Stage
Risograph • Fiction

Germany • *Lahr (Schwarzwald), 07 December 1970*
kontakt@der-roesler.de • **0048 17663716201**

"MOVE MR. MOUNTAIN! (GEH WEG, HERR BERG!)." ATLANTIS. ZURICH. 2018
"ME AND MY FEAR." FLYING EYE BOOKS. LONDON. 2018
"THE JOURNEY." FLYING EYE BOOKS. LONDON. 2016
"EIN LOCH GEGEN DEN REGEN." ATLANTIS. ZURICH. 2016

FRANCESCA SANNA

FRANCESCASANNA.COM

4 EARTH STILLS THE WIND. SO
RED AND ORANGE AND YELLOW
LEAVES FLOAT TO THE GROUND

My Friend Earth

Gouache, ink, digital media • Fiction

Chronicle Books, San Francisco, to be published, ISBN 9780811879101

Italy • *Cagliari, 31 May 1991*

hello@francescasanna.com • 0039 3313184091

EDUARDO SGANGA

BEHANCE.NET/EDUARDOSGANGA

Danubio (Danube) • Digital media • Fiction

Uruguay • *Montevideo, 26 May 1983*

e.sganga@gmail.com • 0059 898717005

1

1-5 DANUBE

1 ONCE UPON A TIME. IN A JUNGLE. THERE WAS A LAKE WITH COOL AND CLEAR WATER. THERE WERE SOME RABBITS LIVING AROUND. WHENEVER THEY WERE THIRSTY. THEY WOULD DRINK THE COOL WATER. THEY HAD A NICE AND CALM LIFE

2 UNTIL A GROUP OF ELEPHANTS CAME TO THAT JUNGLE. THESE ELEPHANTS WOULD COME TO THE LAKE TO DRINK WATER EVERY DAY

3 THE RABBITS COULDN'T DRINK WATER COMFORTABLY ANYMORE AND ON THE OTHER HAND THEY MADE THE WATER DIRTY AND MUDDY

5 THAT NIGHT WAS THE 14TH OF THE MONTH. THE MOON WAS FULL IN THE SKY. THE SMART RABBIT CLIMBED UP THE MOUNTAIN AND SHOUTED: "THE ELEPHANTS CAN'T GET CLOSE TO THE LAKE BECAUSE IT BELONGS TO THE RABBITS!" "I AM THE MESSENGER OF THE MOON." HE SAID.

"THE PARROT AND THE GROCER." THE INSTITUTE FOR RESEARCH ON HISTORY OF CHILDRES'S LITERATURE. TEHRAN. 2019
"SALM. TOUR AND ERAJ. COLLECTION OF SHAHNAMEH STORIES." KHANEH ADABIAT PUBLICATION. TEHRAN. 2015
"THE GUARD OF SUN." THULE EDICIONES. BARCELONA. 2013
"THE GUARD OF SUN." LUK BOOKS. SEOUL. 2013
"THE SMART RABBIT AND NAMA RAVEN." EGITEN COCUK. ANKARA. 2013
"THE TWELVE-VOLUME COLLECTION OF RUMI (PARROT AND THE GROCER)". KANOON. TEHRAN. 2009
"THE RAINBOW OF SHOES." KUNNA BOOKA. SEOUL. 2009
"THE FOX." KUNNA BOOKA. SEOUL. 2009
"THE FOX." SHABAVIZ PUBLICATION. TEHRAN. 2007
"THE SUN GUARDIAN." SHABAVIZ PUBLICATION. TEHRAN. 2007
"A RAINBOW OF SHOES." SHABAVIZ PUBLICATION. TEHRAN. 2006

3

5

AMIR SHABANIPOUR

The Rabbits of the Spring of the Moon

Digital media • Fiction

The Institute for Research on history of Children's Literature in Iran publication,

Tehran, to be published, ISBN 9786226986014

Iran • *Fooman, 22 June 1979*

amirshabanipour@yahoo.com • 0098 09118185431

1

2

 "MICE AND THE CITY: AROUND THE WORLD." THAMES AND HUDSON. LONDON. 2018
"MICE IN THE CITY: NEW YORK." THAMES AND HUDSON. LONDON. 2018

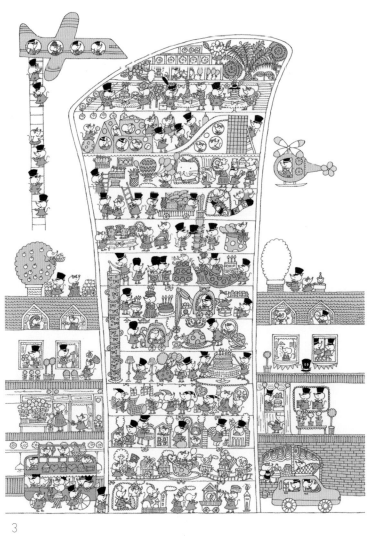

3

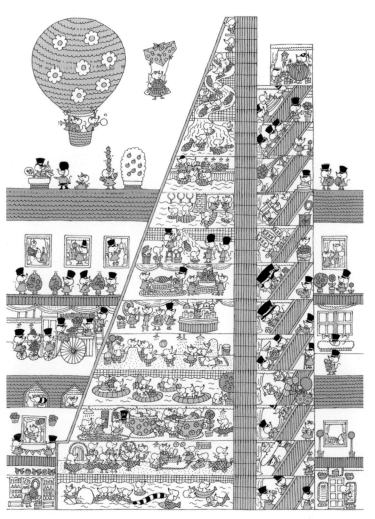

4

1 BIG BEN   2 30ST MARY AXE   3 WALKIE-TALKIE BUILDING   4 THE CHEESEGRATER

AMI SHIN
AMISHIN-ILLUST.COM

Mice in the City: London • Pen, digital media • Fiction
Thames & Hudson Ltd, London, 2018, ISBN 9780500651292
Korea • *Ulsan, 12 June 1983*
jevisatang@gmail.com • 0082 01046634870

1

2

SI PICTURE BOOK SCHOOL
DIRECTOR/COORDINATOR: SUNKYUNG CHO

3

4

1 A GIRL RIDING A BICYCLE IN THE SPRING YELLOW FLOWERS 2 A GIRL RIDING A BICYCLE
IN THE SUMMER RAIN 3 A GIRL RIDING A BICYCLE IN THE AUTUMN FOREST 4 REST AT THE PEAK

HYEJIN SHIN

Bicycle · Watercolor · Fiction

Korea · *Seoul, 07 December 1979*

jinny442@hotmail.com · 0082 1042354420

JUNLI SONG

ARTSOFSONG.COM

Tails of the City

Silkscreen • Fiction

USA • *Berlin, 27 March 1990*

artsofsong@gmail.com • 0044 7084341256

"CHERRY MOON." ZAZA KIDS BOOK IN ASSOCIATION WITH TROIKA BOOKS. LONDON. 2019
"GALILÉE PART EN VRILLE." LES PETITS PLATONS. PARIS. 2019

2

"FOUND IN MELBOURNE." ALLEN & UNWIN. MELBOURNE. 2018
"FOUND IN HONG KONG." PEAK PUBLISHING. HONG KONG. 2015
"THE SWIMMER." PEAK PUBLISHING. HONG KONG. 2014
"CICADA." JOINT PUBLISHING. HONG KONG. 2013

5

KORI SONG
KORISONG.COM

Mountain by the Sea • Pencil, digital media • Fiction

China • *Chongqing, 11 August 1980*

koriillustration@gmail.com • 0085 292648687

4

"PRAŽSKÉ VIZE." PASEKA. PRAGUE. 2018
"SPECIAL CIRCUMSTANCES. AN ILLUSTRATED GUIDE TO DEMOLISHED. REMOVED AND RELOCATED
ART IN PUBLIC SPACE FROM THE PERIOD OF COMMUNISM." PAGE FIVE. FAVU VUT & PAF.
PRAGUE. 2017
"PIONÝŘI A ROBOTI." PASEKA. PRAGUE. 2016

"KAPKY NA KAMENI." ALBATROS MEDIA. PRAGUE. 2019
"PRAŽSKÉ VIZE." PASEKA. PRAGUE. 2018

"JEŽÍŠKOVA KOŠILKA." ALBATROS MEDIA. PRAGUE. 2017

5

JAN ŠRÁMEK & VERONIKA VLKOVÁ

BEHANCE.NET/VJKOLOUCH & BEHANCE.NET/VERONIKAVLKOVA

To je metro, čéče! (That's the Subway, Man!)

Watercolor, digital collage • Nonfiction

Paseka, Prague, 2019, ISBN 9788074329449

Czech Republic • *Prague, 6 October 1983*

koloucholda@seznam.cz • 0042 0606054344

Czech Republic • *Brno, 1 February 1985*

galerieon@gmail.com • 0042 0602963622

"VORN DIE OSTSEE. HINTEN DIE FRIEDRICHSTRAßE."
INSEL-VERLAG. BERLIN. 2019
"VIER KERZEN. DREI KÖNIGE. ZWEI AUGEN. EIN STERN."
PETER HAMMER VERLAG. WUPPERTAL. 2019
"DIE HAUSKATZE IST SELTEN EINE WEIßE." TOLLES HEFT.
BÜCHERGILDE GUTENBERG. FRANKFURT. 2017
"SCHWIMMT BROT IN MILCH?." ALADIN. HAMBURG. 2017
"LUCA AL MUSEO / LUCA AT THE MUSEUM / LUCA IM MUSEUM."
CORRAINI EDIZIONI. MANTOVA. 2016
"STARK WIE EIN BÄR." CARLSEN. HAMBURG. 2011
"I MUSICANTI DI BREMA / THE MUSICIANS OF BREMEN"
CORRAINI EDIZIONI. MANTOVA. 2009

KATRIN STANGL
KATRINSTANGL.DE

Germany • *Filderstadt, 05 May 1977*

illustration@katrinstangl.de • 0049 221679920

Tous au vert! (All Green!)

Ink, digital media • Fiction

Éditions Sarbacane, Paris, 2019, ISBN 9782377312985

4

"LE PARC DE MARGUERITE." EDITIONS NOTARI. GENÈVE. 2015
"LE TIGRI DI MOMPRACEM." ELI READERS. LORETO. 2014

SARA STEFANINI

SARASTEFANINI.COM

Imaginary Friends

Brush pen, pen, colored pencils • Fiction

Switzerland • *Sorengo, 22 June 1982*

stefanini.sara@gmail.com • 0039 3408101050

3 DO YOU BELIEVE HE LIKES GUMMY BEARS?
4 SHE IS THE FASTEST IN THE WORLD

2

3

5

RACHEL STUBBS

RACHELCELIASTUBBS.COM

My Red Hat

Graphite, ink, digital media • Fiction

Walker Books, London, 2020, ISBN 9781406380668

United Kingdom • *Bury St. Edmunds, 13 December 1984*

rachelceliastubbs@gmail.com • 0044 7716931970

4

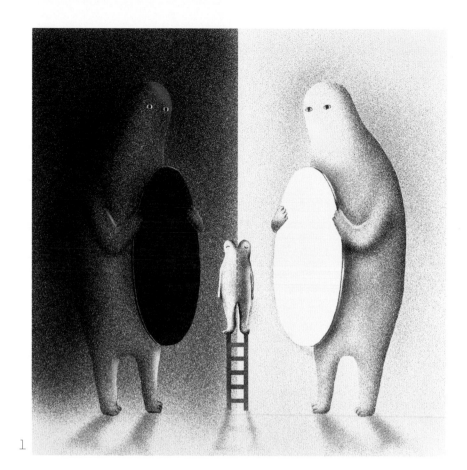

1

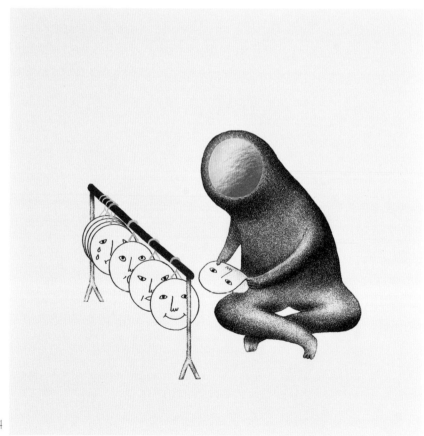

4

2

LU WEN TING

Dotted Line • Mixed media • Fiction

Taiwan • *New Taipei City, 03 April 1990*

christine1293@gmail.com • 0088 6917549979

2

"HOW TO RAISE A CHILD WHO NEVER GIVES UP." PHP INSTITUTE. TOKYO. 2006
"HOW TO RAISE A RIGHT-HEARTED CHILD - SMALL HABITS AND HOME
DISCIPLINES IN CHILD REARING". PHP INTSITUTE. TOKYO. 2001

2 THEY FIND VARIOUS LIGHTS IN THE FOREST. "WHAT'S THAT?" "MIGHT BE THE GUIDE" 4 YAPONE SEES A RAY OF LIGHT SHINING THROUGH

NINUKI TSUJI

ATELIERNINUKI.WIXSITE.COM/NINUKI

Apon and Yapone. The Story of the Beginning of the Witches

Etching, aquatint, drypoint • Fiction

Japan • *Kyoto City, 23 November 1963*

atelier.ninuki@gmail.com • 0081 9021951825

JUAN CRISTÓBAL VERA GIL

JUANCRIS.COM

City Gets Better • Colored pencils • Fiction

Spain • *Solingen, 24 January 1973*

hello@juancris.com • 0034 619226920

INÊS VIEGAS OLIVEIRA
IVOLIVEIRA.COM

So Many Things

Oil, watercolor, collage, pencils, digital media • Fiction

Portugal • *Tavira, 02 March 1995*

olineso11@gmail.com • 0035 1914242181

1

2

4

5

1 ON THE ROAD   2 BERLIN   4 NEW FRIENDS   5 IRELAND

KATERINA VORONINA

KATEVORONINA.COM

Migratory Birds

Acrylic, colored pencils, collage • Fiction

Russia • *Volgograd, 28 July 1988*

voroninakaterin@gmail.com • 0049 15225484856

4

"MIGRANTES." ED. LOS LIBROS DEL ZORRO ROJO. BARCELONA. 2018
"MÀS TE VALE. MASTODONTE." ED. FCE MÉXICO. CIUDAD DE MEXICO. 2014
"LAS PEQUEÑAS AVENTURAS DE JUANITO Y SU BICICLETA AMARILLA."
POLIFONÍA. LIMA. 2013

ISSA WATANABE

Ausencia (Absence)

Mixed media • Fiction

Peru • *Lima, 21 February 1980*

watanabeissa@gmail.com • 0051 1977363494

KATE WINTER

KATEWINTER.NET
INSTAGRAM.COM/KATEWINTERFREELAND

20.000 Years Ago They Found a Cave
Mixed media • Nonfiction
Penguin Random House, London, to be published
United Kingdom • *Cambridge, 21 March 1977*
katewinter77@gmail.com • 0044 07977468363

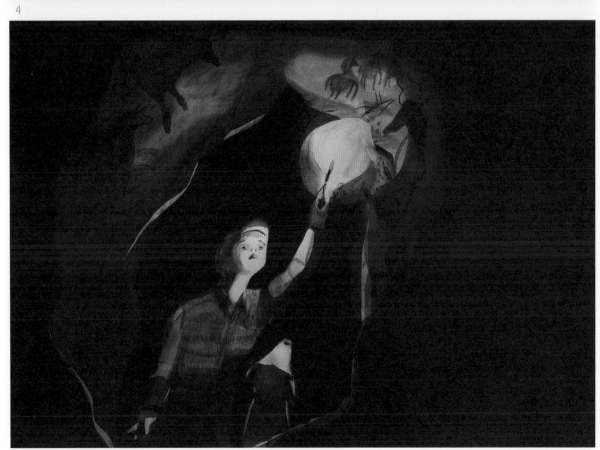

"OIL PASTEL DRAWING SKILLS—THE DETAILED ANNOTATION OF WU PENG'S ILLUSTRATION." HUBEI FINE ARTS PUBLISHING HOUSE, WUHAN CITY, 2017

1

PENG WU

ILLUSTRATORWUPENG.COM

A Travel • Gouache, colored pencil, collage, digital media • Fiction

China • *Taiyuan Shanxi, 04 January 1987*

wupengchocolate@gmail.com • 0086 17601655080

2

3

4

5

WANXIN WU

A Cat In a Box

China ink, pencil • Fiction

China • *Jiang Su, 22 January 1987*

wanxin.wu@gmail.com • 0081 5053180469

5

"LITTLE PERO (LITTLE LICKY RIDING HOOD)." SHOUGAKUKAN. TOKYO. 2019
"LITTLE PERO DOUBUTSU-ENSOKU (LITTLE LICKY RIDING HOOD AT THE ZOO)."
SHOUGAKUKAN. TOKYO. 2019
"A-I-U-E-WO-N." PARADEBOOKS. OSAKA. 2014
"MERRY-GO-ROUND NO CHIISANA UMA TAI NI." GENTOSHA. TOKYO. 2012

MAMORU YAMAMOTO
MAMORUYAMAMOTO.COM

Little Moja
Colored pencil, digital media • Fiction
Japan • *Tokyo, 10 November 1960*
mamoroll@purple.plala.or.jp • 0081 9071911964

1

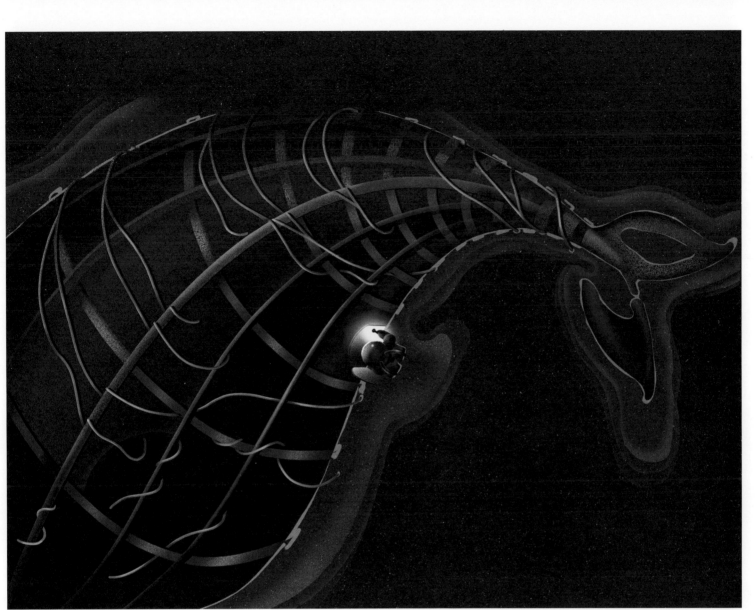

3

YASHIN

YASHINSTUDIO.CPM

Deeper Blue

Digital media • Fiction

Self published, Taiwan, 2019, ISBN 9789574371402

Taiwan • *Miaoli, 09 January 1990*

yayashin1990@gmail.com • 0088 6919624522

3

KANGMI YOON

A Building Where Trees Grow
Gouache, collage, colored pencils, digital media • Fiction
Changbi publishers, Gyeonggi-do, 2019, ISBN 9788936455354 77810

Korea • *Gyeongsan, 02 October 1966*

ylala@naver.com • 0082 1036328932

AND THROUGH DRAWING NOT ONLY DO I AMUSE MYSELF. BUT I ALSO LEARN. I GRASP THE WORLD.

MARISCAL

JAVIER MARISCAL (Valencia, 1950) describes his life as "a love story with drawing." An illustrator, designer, creator of comics, graphic artist, painter, sculptor and landscape architect, he has also worked on animated films and multimedia art. His illustrations have appeared on the covers of publications like "The New Yorker," "El País" and the Japanese magazine "Apo." He has received international prizes and honors for a wide range of pursuits: from art to illustration, design to cinema.

You are a truly multidisciplinary artist, as critics like to say. How does your work as an illustrator influence your work as a designer, and vice versa?

I was born with a somewhat flawed mind; later I discovered I was dyslexic and dyscalculic, and for my whole life, since I have been able to reason, I have rummaged around in that big cabinet where there is a drawer called illustration, another called architecture, and art, painting, cinema, design, lettering . . . I take that cabinet, tip it over and mix up everything. I cannot do otherwise. I know that one ought to keep things separate: this is architecture, this is illustration, this is design . . . But things are not really like that. When you walk in the forest, everything has a continuous relationship with its surroundings: if a tree sways in the wind, it causes changes around it. The fact of the matter is that everything is crossed by human language, and often this language is not rational but graphic, emotional and poetic. This is why I cannot tell you if my illustration has influenced my way of doing design and vice versa, because for me it is all one whole. All my work, in the end, always comes from a drawing on a piece of paper (or directly on a computer, it makes no difference); then from that initial concept, I begin to work. On colors, for example, a highly symbolic languages that goes directly to feelings: red is a color full of life, but it can also be a color of death; yellow is the color of light, but it can also be the color of an illness. It depends on how you use it and how you mix it, to convey one meaning or another. To some extent, my work consists of organizing information. You make a flyer and people understand if there is an exhibition of furniture, or a concert of music. Through colors and fonts, the information can be made clearer, easier to decipher. The graphic language is very important, because communication through symbols is intrinsic to human beings. If we were to take away all the symbols and all the graphic elements, there would be total chaos, because no one would know which button to push for play, or how to get to the airport.

In everything you do, your style is always very recognizable. Whether it's an illustration, the design of a logo, an animated film, a piece of furniture or a work of art, it is almost always possible to say: "Mariscal made this." Is this recognition something you consciously seek, or does it just happen? I always try to change register, but the truth is that in the end, everything I do resembles me somehow. Once I saw a little boy below one of my sculptures, a giant shrimp that hangs over a bar in Barcelona. He gazed at the shrimp and said: "Look, it's Cobi!" *[the mascot of the Barcelona Olympics in 1992 designed by Mariscal in 1987, ed]*. It made me laugh. Now that I am 70 years old, when they ask me, I say I am an illustrator, but I continue to think that I do it because I have to find some way to pass the time. I like doing nothing, but "doing nothing" is not something you can do every day. So I draw. And through drawing—always drawing, because it was very hard for me to learn to read and write—not only do I amuse myself, but I also learn, I grasp the world. I remember that in the early 1960s my parents brought a moka coffeemaker from Italy, and the first thing I did was to draw it. When I had drawn it, in all its parts, I said to myself: I've got it, it's mine. Even today I feel amazed that the things I do reach so many people, that in the end I get paid for having fun. And at the same time, I understand why in the great Spanish museums there are no works of mine, I think that's right, I'm a guy for the newsstands. I don't complain, in fact I live well doing what I like to do, and I receive a great deal of affection. Recently someone told me: I have a painting of yours in my room, and every morning when I see it, I have the desire to live. I really liked that—no one has ever told me something so beautiful.

In your view, is there a clear difference between working for kids and working for an adult audience?
It makes no difference to me, because a central factor in all my work is precisely play. Playing is not frowned upon in the tradition of design. Using play, which is the first language we learn as kids, is very important. Ettore Sottsass played constantly, as did Achille Castiglioni, just to cite two examples. I always try to introduce elements of play in design and communication. Then, however, you get to college and they tell you to stop: "this is no longer an airplane from World War I, it is a lighter." First you played with it—*tatatatatatata!*—and flames came out of the plane. Then, in college, they tell you to cut it out: it's not a game, it's reality! But we are symbolic animals, I insist on this point. Not that we are more intelligent than an octopus or a whale, we just have this language that has allowed us to construct a very complex society, to ask ourselves who we are and where we come from, and to realize that it is not the sun that spins around the Earth, but vice versa.

Is there an illustrated book, a comic, film, etc. that you discovered as a child, and has somehow remained in your imagination as an illustrator?

Oh, there are so many things, tons of them. *Little Nemo*, Disney films, the Gitane cigarette package, the label on bottles of Cinzano, the covers by Saul Steinberg, thousands of comics, advertising. I saw four-color printing as it first evolved, and when I was 21 years old a new technology was born, the photocopy. Then came electric typewriters, then computers. I have always lived surrounded by images, which have always fascinated me. I discovered Cubism through the figurines they gave you with chocolates, but I also devoured Spanish comics, really thousands of images. At a certain point I discovered Saul Steinberg, and a whole world was opened up for me, as happened with Sottsass. When I discovered the Gitane package on my first trip to France, it was an almost sacred experience. Then came Pop Art, Formica, neon, the Cinquecento, the Vespa . . . I was born in a society where cars were black coffins, furnishings were all dark, in the "remordimiento" style, so when all these other things came along it was simply amazing!

First published in the United States of America in 2020
by Chronicle Books LLC.

Originally published in Italy in 2020 by Maurizio
Corraini s.r.l.

ILLUSTRATORS ANNUAL 2020

Book design
PIETRO CORRAINI
& CORRAINISTUDIO

Translations
EUGENIA DURANTE
STEPHANIE JOHNSON
MARIA TOLOMELLI
TRANSITING SAS
GABRIELLA VERDI
TON VILALTA

Image processing
PUNTO 3 SERVIZI GRAFICI S.R.L. VERONA

ISBN 978-1-4521-6363-5

Manufactured in China.

MIX
Paper from
responsible sources
FSC™ C020056

Interior design by Pietro Corraini & corrainiStudio.
Cover design by Jay Marvel.
Typeset in ARGN and Rooney.

10 9 8 7 6 5 4 3 2 1

CHRONICLE BOOKS LLC
680 SECOND STREET
SAN FRANCISCO, CALIFORNIA 94107

CHRONICLE BOOKS—we see things differently.
Become part of our community at www.chroniclebooks.com.